# BOTTOM HALF TEENS

## A Caring Community-Driven Solution Designed to Rescue Young Lives Trapped in a Broken System



A. JOHN WILEY, JR.

ISBN: 978-1-7336188-0-9 (Paperback)

Library of Congress Control Number: 2019901392

Front cover and book design by Jacob Yahnke

*Printed in the United States of America.*

First printing edition 2019.

10 9 8 7 6 5 4 3 2 1

PUBLISHER
Bottom Half Teens, LLC
500 Moasis Drive
Little Chute, Wisconsin 54140

For information and/or to order single or group purchases, go to **www.bottomhalfteens.com**.

# DEDICATION

This book is dedicated to the millions of U.S. children who didn't ask to be in the "Bottom Half" and need our communities to lend them a hand to raise them up and earn their way out of the "Bottom Half."

With thanks to...

> David Payne, who gifted me with his organizing and editing skills. He was of incredible help to me in taking my many pages of notes/ideas and helping me to develop the concepts in a way that makes this book readable. David, my most sincere and grateful "thank you"!

Special thanks for helping me to understand the "Bottom Half" in Wisconsin's Fox Cities to the following:

> Ed Dwyer - *Waukesha Teacher & Mentor*
> Dennis Kral - *Enterprise Partner,*
> *Wisconsin School Consultive Services*
> Greg Lemke-Rochan - *Fox Cities Boys and Girls Club*
> John Weyenberg - *Habitat for Humanity*
> Kristy Cover - *Habitat for Humanity*
> Joe Mauthe - *Pillars*
> Shawn Robinson - *Dr. Dyslexia Dude*
> *(Wei LAB - UW Madison)*
> Rev. Alvin DuPree - *Pastor at Family First Alliance*

# DEDICATION (CONTINUED)

I would also like to thank the members of the Oshkosh Chamber of Commerce, especially Leo Musa, Bob Fick, and Henry Kimberly, who taught me way back in 1969-70 how a community comes together to attract an organization like the EAA to Oshkosh. And I can't forget the Neenah-Menasha Chamber members who worked on the consolidation of the municipal sewage and paper mill issue, and Bill Kellett who chaired the effort in 1970-75 to merge the communities of Neenah and Menasha into a single community. Even though we lost the political battle in the worst defeat I've ever witnessed, we managed to bring together a deep understanding of each others community municipal and educational issues. From these two Chamber relationships, I learned how to effectively approach community issues.

Finally, I owe deep thanks to Matthew Desmond, the author of *Evicted*, whose book helped me understand what poverty looks and feels like. And to the hundreds of Fox Cities teens and adults who were kind enough to talk to me, share their experiences, and who are living their lives in the "Bottom Half."

# WHO IS JOHN WILEY?

John Wiley is on a late-in-life mission to throw a safety net to teenagers that he believes are on the road to a lifetime of poverty, kids who feel a disconnect at school and who do not find themselves properly prepared to work in America's 21st century computer based economy.

In his new book, "Our Bottom Half Teens: A Caring Community-Driven Solution Designed to Rescue Young Lives Trapped in a Broken System," Wiley lays out a plan that includes a massive expansion of apprenticeship programs in high schools, calling on businesses and schools to collaborate to give students the ability to opt into a paid apprenticeship program as early as their sophomore year.

"Bottom Half Teens" might not be the most politically correct term, Wiley admits, but it's one that gets the point across. Those students who are unmotivated in school and whose grades put them in the bottom half of their class with little desire to improve need another option. The apprenticeship track gives them that option, the chance to learn a skill and get workplace training (while earning money) so they are ready to work full time and succeed after high school.

"You can't not give kids a chance," Wiley says. "Every kid needs to be loved, every kid needs to be important, every kid needs to be valued. Every kid needs those things."

**So, who is John Wiley?**

The 76-year-old Appleton, Wisconsin teacher-turned-entrepreneur-turned-activist has founded and run several companies, worked as an executive at two chambers of commerce, helped launch a Boys and Girls Club in his beloved Fox Valley, chaired a juvenile violence task force and worked hand in hand with the Salvation Army for a decade and a half.

Two years ago he was so inspired by Matthew Desmond's book, "Evicted: Poverty and Profit in the American City," that he spent his own money to purchase and distribute hundreds of copies of the books to Fox Valley community leaders, business leaders and others in hopes that they, too, would see and act on the need for more affordable housing and other life lines for those who struggle to stay afloat.

Following that experience, he began writing a series of essays about how we're failing the "bottom half" kids, pushing a significant percentage of teens through high school knowing the bleakness that awaits once they are adults. Those essays led to his new book. He hopes it's the beginning of a new conversation, a grassroots movement with buy-in from the students, their parents, the schools and employers.

"It has to be the community," Wiley says of addressing these issues. "It's not the school's fault. It's not the police department's fault. It's the community that has to do these things. As citizens, we have responsibilities. The Democrats all say the government should do it. The Republicans say let everyone fend for themselves. It isn't them. It's us. It's our standards, it's our values that allow this to happen."

Wiley has lived out a career as an entrepreneur in Wisconsin. His "working" career began teaching "slow learners" and "discipline problems" for four years in Waukesha, Wisconsin. He would later run the Oshkosh and Neenah-Menasha chambers of commerce for seven years, help found and build Outlook Graphics for 34 years, and own Elipticon Wood Products for 24 years.

He has been an active member of the Rotary Club for 45 years, serving as the District Governor in 1994-1995. His passion to serve disadvantaged families and children led him to serve on the board of the Salvation Army for 14 years. In addition, he was instrumental in developing Project Home and with others in starting a day-care alternative high school in Wautoma, Wisconsin and a 24/7 care alternative high school in Reedsville, Wisconsin.

He also chaired the Mayor's Juvenile Violence Task Force, the Chamber of Commerce's Apprenticeship Program in the 1990s, and Fox Valley Lutheran High School's Blue Ribbon Committee and Funding a Fresh Start Committee, all in Appleton.

Wiley has been married for 51 years to his wife, Sandy, and has been blessed with four children: Nell, Ben, Ladd, and Rica along with his 10 "sparkling" grandchildren.

## A SALUTE TO DAVE PAYNE

John invited Dave, as a friend, to read Evicted. John then shared his plan for this book. Dave grew up in the Fox Cities. His dad Spencer was the first person in his family to attend college ... a wonderful gift from the Kimberly family who paid Spencer's way to graduate from Lawrence College. It's a story that surely fits the message of this book about what it means to be a friend to those in the "Bottom Half." Dave enjoyed the opportunity to meet regularly with John about his book project and to experience John's passion to "be a friend" for those who truly need a voice in our society. "As John penned page after page, it was my pleasure to help him develop and more clearly organize his writing. Thank you, John, for being a friend and giving me the opportunity to think deeply about this important subject."

# TABLE OF CONTENTS

# TABLE OF CONTENTS

# TABLE OF CONTENTS

## ALL CHILDREN NEED TO...

Have a friend.
Be a friend.
Be valued.
Be respected.
Feel worthwhile.
Be safe.
Be included.
Be important.
Be successful.
Be needed.
Have hope for their future.
Have their own American dream.

This is true at home, at school, in their neighborhood, and in their work.

All of us can avoid lots of problems when teens are valued and have a positive sense of self.

It gives me great peace and joy to present this book and these thoughts to you.

# CHAPTER 1

## Students in Pain!

It is very painful to observe how students in poverty or with disparities are treated in schools today ... especially in the Fox Cities' schools.

**"Bottom Half" students** are not being educated to find success in the adult world. These valuable lives represent the people who will operate our machines at work and provide services to the community for years to come. They are the base of the standard of living in our Fox Cities' communities.

"Bottom Half" students are generally not engaged nor enthused about their schooling.

What is to be done?

This book provides an entrepreneurial approach to have the Fox Cities' communities make things right. It offers a practical approach offering teens a focused pathway to success through the world of work and their lives outside of work.

Correctly implemented, this plan would thoroughly increase enthusiasm and opportunity for Fox Cities teens currently being underserved in the "Bottom Half" of our community. It offers reduced stress, increased productivity, a place to belong, and earn respect and dignity. It provides the chance to significantly reduce negative behaviors including alcohol and drug abuse, violence, teen pregnancy, depression and mental stress over their uncertain futures.

Even more, we wouldn't need private funding or Federal dollars to make this happen. This proposal empowers our teens in the "Bottom Half" to take a meaningful place in society. This plan would fill current Fox Cities labor shortages with qualified workers ready to grasp their part of the American Dream.

# CHAPTER 2

## Observing Education Today

This book is not a product of extensive academic research. After years of observing our struggling students and schools, I am convinced we don't need another academic study. To me, the current thinking of educators is misplaced. Education today is missing the key purposes or reasons behind public education:

**REASON #1:**

Children need to be educated so that they can transition from their lives as students to become engaged citizens, capable and qualified as workers who are able to adjust to the changing technologies and methods that will occur during their lifetimes.

**REASON #2:**

Education is for all people poor, rich, bright, challenged or otherwise. Historically, our forefathers wanted primary and secondary education to serve as a free means for the youth of our nation to have a fair chance to move out of poverty into a decent, safe, and sanitary standard of living. They desired for the young people to be trained to work successfully and take their part in a thriving community.

**REASON #3:**

Communication and cooperation between the home and school is not efficient or effective. Teamwork between parents and teachers is limited, resulting in lower educational productivity for the children. Parents and teachers need to work together and develop mutual goals for child values growth. Often home and school values are in conflict with each other. Social growth needs to connect at home and at school.

My observation during a lifetime of working with disadvantaged people is that our current education system does not serve poor people well. Matthew Desmond's impactful book "Evicted" opened my eyes to these inadequacies. Three years of talking to individuals and observing poverty and education in Wisconsin's Fox Cities has solidified my view that we need to find a new and better way to serve these "Bottom Half" families.

In my estimation, the "Bottom Half" of our high school students are not serious about their education because they find little relevancy to their "real life" goals and situations. They are allowed to drift through classes uninterested and unmotivated. The focus is more on maintaining adequate behavior standards and maintaining achievement goals that will keep funding flowing to the schools. This has little relevance to the students who are struggling to find a successful place in life and the adult community that is waiting for them upon graduation.

*My observation during a lifetime of working with disadvantaged people is that our current education system does not serve poor people well.*

I am suggesting a number of fundamental cultural changes which, if adopted by our communities, would provide a more relevant education and would retool the way we currently educate the "Bottom Half" of our students. The ideas proposed in this book can be accomplished without significant increases in spending, but does require a re-allocation of resources to "do education" more efficiently and effectively.

I believe we can change the amount and depth of poverty in the Fox Cities by simply educating our youth to be capable workers, trained and transitioned to be successful in the world of work throughout their lifetimes. Our goal in the Fox Cities needs to be to produce the best trained work force in America and the entire world.

It is my hope that this book will not only produce a healthy community dialogue, but also that it will stimulate substantive changes in the effectiveness of Fox Cities' education to better serve "Bottom Half" students and their families.

While I have focused on the Fox Cities in Wisconsin, communities across the USA can drive community wide discussions to evaluate and improve education and the adult quality of life and work for their "Bottom Half Teens."

Nearly **1 in 5 children under 6 were poor** and almost half of them **lived in extreme poverty.**

- Children's Defense Fund

# CHAPTER 3:

## Making the "Grade" in Our Schools

Before moving beyond the issue of schools, I think it is important to address the way the current grading system discourages student productivity. Grading high school students with D's, F's, and even C's seems to me to de-motivate rather than motivate students today. Instead of a focus on letter grades and "better" grades, which essentially only motivates the most academically gifted students, the focus should be switched to fairly evaluating each student's strengths and weaknesses.

It would be much more meaningful for students for "grading" to begin with self-evaluation. In this way, each student can gauge their success in reaching both their personal goals and the values of the community.

*Grading high school students with D's, F's, and even C's seems to me to de-motivate rather than motivate students today.*

At best, grades measure classroom proficiency over specific coursework. Unfortunately, those simple letters do little beyond that and are weak indicators of future success in real-life situations. There is an entire curriculum outside the class work that needs be considered.

I like to refer to them as "community values." Qualities like . . .

- Fairness
- Honesty
- Respect
- Accountability
- Service
- Humanity
- Problem-solving
- Justice
- Protecting the weak
- Capable workers
- Effective parents
- Good Citizens

Governments don't set these "community values"; nor do school boards. It is a fabric of life in the community of the high school and reflects the values of the residents and businesses located in that community with their unique population base. See Chapters 41-44 for further development of the values grading concept.

# CHAPTER 4:

## On the Record ... Police Record

I hope that you are as shocked as I am that in 2016 in Wisconsin 9.291% of our teens age 10-17 were arrested. That is a shocking statistic!

You can argue that the statistics are skewed by Milwaukee and its surrounding area, but something is very wrong in our state. That means 56,054 of our teens were arrested. That is the size of a city!

The next closest state was Wyoming at just over 7%, but only 4,144 teens. Still too many, but a far cry from 56,054. The U.S. national average for arrests of teens in this age range is just over 3%. Something is very wrong.

Add to that the fact that the U.S. arrests more people than most other nations in the world. Wisconsin might likely have the highest arrest rate for young people on our globe! When it comes to arrests, New York State, which has at least as many challenges as Wisconsin, is second lowest with only a 1.261% arrest rate. Wisconsin arrests seven times more of our teens than New York State does annually per capita.

What happens when a teen is arrested? In Wisconsin, plenty. Plenty that the average person may not even realize. For children under age 16, that child now has "a record" that can follow them during their life. For these young offenders, it is a not a public record, but police, the courts, lawyers, and prosecutors have access to that young person's arrest record to establish a pattern of behavior.

For teens age 17 or older who are arrested, this information goes on their permanent record that can be accessed not only by the courts and law enforcement, but also by employers, colleges, the military and any other interested persons. This is serious. Obviously, arrests are consequential and may have a huge bearing on a teen's future. It will affect their self-image and the image they present to others, perhaps for a lifetime.

Again, I ask: Why is Wisconsin leading our nation, and perhaps the whole world, in arrests of children ages 10-17? Why seven times the rate of New York state? Why 56,000 teens?

This is an issue for our entire state. We, as taxpayers, pay for this "lock 'em up" attitude. In our state, we pay three times more for incarceration than we do for education. A cynic might argue that we are better at teaching our teens how to become adult criminals and to "do time."

Before we in the Fox Cities look accusingly at the "big" cities of Milwaukee, Madison, and Green Bay, it would be good to look at our records for juvenile arrests. In my mind, there are far too many. This book suggests a better answer than arrests. It proposes a positive program that builds skills and self-esteem – the Fox Cities Apprenticeship Action Plan.

One of my friends is a well known retired Fox Cities Public Official. Recently, He and I and some friends were at our Friday lunch when we began to talk about our youthful adventures. He told a story about how he and his High School buddies would go to the park with a couple of cases of beer. Around 10:30 a squad car would pull up and 2 cops would come over and have a beer with these High Schoolers. When they left, they would say "make sure you clean up when you leave."

My oh my how things have changed in 50 years. What would have changed in his life if he had been arrested 2 or 3 times.

Schools, police and Juvenile court can't be places just for punishment. We need to develop positive alternatives.

Wisconsin and Washington are both moving towards expunging arrest records and time served for non-violent crimes. This helps. But, why arrest in the first place. Why are there not more constructive alternatives to arrests and perhaps jail time?

# CHAPTER 5:

## Take a Closer Look at "Our" Fox Cities

Nestled just south of the "Great Northwoods" of Wisconsin is the Fox River Valley. Settled in the mid-1800's, it offered many families an opportunity to create their version of the American Dream. From its early fur-trading routes, to woodenwares, to the paper industry, bookbinding, and so much more, these communities brought to life the dream of finding success to immigrants of many nationalities. In Appleton, Neenah-Menasha, Kimberly, Kaukauna, Little Chute, Combined Locks, and surrounding townships, families fulfilled their dream of owning their own home and establishing a stable standard of living for themselves and their children.

Today these communities have grown to a combined population of over a quarter million. Served by solid education systems, the Fox Cities boasts eleven high schools to prepare teens for the future. Shopping, industry, health care and public service all offer ample opportunities for families of the Fox River Valley.

A little piece of "paradise"? Perhaps. But let's take closer look...

Our Fox Cities community is the most important place in our lives. It is where we live. It is where we work. It is our neighbors, our friends, and our future. Together, we are better than we ever could be on our own.

From my vantage point, however, I see a major weakness. We are not always cognizant of our entire community. It is easy to focus on the successful among us, but there are many who struggle. Consider the number of children who need to eat breakfast or lunch in our schools. The statistics in our quaint Midwestern community may astound you. Nearly half live in marginal income households which means their support is in jeopardy from paycheck to paycheck. Looking closer, this figure includes 13% of our Fox Cities children who live below the poverty line and an additional 29%, who according to ALICE's (Asset Limited, Income Constrained, Employed) county statistics, face great challenges daily. (For a detailed view of these ALICE statistics for Fox Cities counties, refer to the Appendix section on page 153.)

You may say that those who are struggling are the ones who receive the most financial assistance. Healthy communities, however, understand that these people need more than a handout. They need a "hand up." I believe the Fox Cities is one of the best places to live in all America. Solid schools, employment opportunities, strong nonprofits, effective government: all these are simply the beginning of the positive assets people of the Fox Cities enjoy.

We need to pay more attention to what I call the "Bottom Half" of our communities and in particular the children of "Bottom Half" families. As a former employer, I have been touched by the lives of the workers that I have come to know in my different community roles. These are good people who can make a way for themselves. I found that the more we, as employers, paid attention to them as individuals, the more they cared about "their" company, its products, and the quality of their work.

I believe that community leaders and partners can do much to end the cycle of poverty for many in the "Bottom Half Teens," by thoughtfully extending a "hand-up" through apprenticeships, teaching productive work experiences and skills.

In the 90's I was chairman of the Fox Cities Apprenticeship program for 2 years. At Outlook Graphics, where I worked, we had 3 apprentices each year, on a 2 year program. These teens were practiced, experienced and fully qualified to run the 40" 6-color press. The going rate at that time was $40,000-50,000 per year, in the 90's. We can do that type of thing again!

# CHAPTER 6

## Milwaukee's Poverty – How Far Away from Life in the Fox Cities?

After reading "Evicted" by Matthew Desmond, I wanted to challenge my fellow citizens of the Fox Cities to read this troubling book so that they could get a mental picture of poverty in Milwaukee's slums and come to see that some of those same conditions exist here in the Fox River Valley.

As I handed out hundreds of copies and had hundreds of conversations about the trap of poverty. I began to see from the stories people told me about themselves and their families a little bit more about the cycle of poverty. One of the frequent problems mentioned was that about half of our high school-aged teens were reasonably well behaved, but not engaged in their education. As such, these young men and women had only a loosely defined purpose in life and few real goals for their own future. The consequences point to young adult lives that are poorly prepared for the challenges of work, family life, and successful citizenship after high school graduation.

This change comes upon these high school age teens abruptly. Suddenly, they are out of the education world and thrust into the need to find a promising job with a future. Their high school experience with hours of daily "after school" idle time from 3:00 - 6:00 p.m. and long summer vacations leaves them ill-prepared to step into the new schedule of life after graduation. Employers need employees with experience, qualifications and skills.

Many low income parents reported difficulty in reaching out to teachers or administrators in the school setting to get the help they felt they needed for their teens. These parents felt this lack of communication definitely affected the education and ultimate lifestyles they found their children enter as adults. The Children's Defense Fund (CDF) promotes spending 40% more per person for "Bottom Half" students. (See CDF Report in Appendix, pages 173-188)

This communication impasse is not necessarily the fault of the schools, but rather points to a need to look at the purpose and structure of our current education system as well as to evaluate the satisfaction we feel about the status quo of education in the Fox Cities.

I am recommending a more European approach to education. It is a style of education that prepares their young people to embrace their future and to actively pursue this career preparation as a central focus of education. This focus can already begin at the kindergarten or preschool level. For example, the Montessori model teaches that play is a child's work. They begin at an early age to set examples and habits. Little ones are free to play with any toy in the classroom, but when the child is finished playing with that toy, it is their responsibility to put the toy away. This is primary preparation for the world of work they will experience years in the future. Effective parents follow this same model and reinforce this life skill at home. This partnership of parents, especially "Bottom Half" parents, and schools on the primary life skills is vital.

This book suggests that we in the Fox Cities reorganize our schools and build partnerships with both employers and parents in a coordinated effort to engage children of all ages in their own education and future. This is especially key for teens beginning at the age of thirteen or fourteen in the "Bottom Half."

Employers should and do play a major role in training employees to work productively in ways that increase customer satisfaction. Employee efforts play a tremendous role in customer satisfaction. This focused process can begin with students engaged in apprenticeship programs already in the early teen years and can continue as they move to full-time employees in their twenties. I believe that young employees need to be educated two to three years beyond high school to ages 21-23 in order to be more able to grow with the rapidly changing technology of today's work world.

Wise employers will provide partial scholarships for their capable young employees into their twenties to continue schooling at settings like Fox Valley Technical College, which has a wonderful working model, and also the newly reorganized state college system formerly known as the Fox Valley Center of the University of Wisconsin (now under the leadership of UW-Oshkosh.) This would be the best way to prepare apprentices and future employees to step into meaningful and changing roles in industry and employment. This proposal does suggest this change to Fox Cities' culture to carefully prepare future workers for work now and for the foreseeable future.

Consider the value of having our Fox Cities' teens graduate from high school with a job they are fully prepared and trained to do. Think about how much better this approach to education will be for average high school graduates. Think about how much better it will be for these same students as they learn about the process of applying for, being hired for, and keeping jobs they want.

*Young employees need to be educated two to three years beyond high school in order to be more able to grow with the rapidly changing technology of today's work world.*

From an economic standpoint, I believe this proposal is revenue neutral. Any displacement of teachers should be absorbed as "job liaisons" working with schools, students, employers, and "Bottom Half" parents. More on this comes later in the book.

This Fox Cities Youth Apprenticeship Program will provide employers with 6,600,000 annual hours of work by employing an average of 200 high school students from grades 10-12 in each of our 11 high schools. That is an eventual total of 2,200 apprentices being prepared to join the Fox Cities work force per year.

If we use the round figure of a wage of $10 per hour, this means that this program can provide "Bottom Half" families or students with $10,000 annual incomes for 1000 hours of work, five hours per day for 200 days each year. Those apprentices receiving a round figure of $10,000 in wages each year would be a $66,000,000 impact on the disadvantaged "Bottom Half" and their families ... and ultimately the economy of the Fox Cities as well.

Teaching these apprentices, indeed all teens, the principles of money management, saving, investing, and real life budgeting in school would be another major impact. For example, if each apprentice would invest one tenth of their income each year for five years beginning at age 15, and would hold it in a Roth IRA following Warren Buffet index fund concept, they would have $1,161,581 at age 65.

Could this be a voluntary condition of employment in the apprenticeship program that each teen save ten percent of their income and invest in index funds as Warren Buffet did in his famous $1M bet with Wall Street fund managers? All would be millionaires by their mid-sixties! (Details are found in the chapter entitled "The Rule of 72," page 135)

Big thoughts. Big impacts. All produced simply by teaching teens how to work five hours per day for 200 days per year. These are big changes for teen mental health and educational focus. These are big changes for employers with an influx of new employees with effective job experience and training.

Let's make Fox Cities education relevant for the "Bottom Half" of our students.

# CHAPTER 7

## Who is the "Bottom Half"?

The term "Bottom Half" itself sounds a little insulting, doesn't it? Who wants to be in the "Bottom Half." Not me. Probably not you. Would you want your children to be characterized as being in the "Bottom Half" of their class?

In reality, all of us are in the "Bottom Half" in some aspects of our lives. Maybe you are never going to be a top-flight golfer. Maybe your reading or comprehension skills are not strong. Maybe you would rather die than get up in front of a group of people and speak. Maybe your mechanical skills make using a hammer or screwdriver a life-threatening activity. Not everyone is good at everything. And that is okay.

Half of the people in America are in the "Bottom Half." Half were in the "Bottom Half" when they were born. Half were in the "Bottom Half" based on their experience in school. Half are in the "Bottom Half" right now based on their earning power, housing situation, or other economic factors. Our communities need to engage our "Bottom Half." We can raise their standard of living. We can raise the value, purpose, and the sense of belonging they can enjoy in this great nation we call America.

"Bottom Half Teens" are not measured by intelligence, more often they are measured by the level of engagement or previously learned competence.

Please understand: there is great power and opportunity in the "Bottom Half." While schools and pop psychology push us to be "our best," the truth is that not everyone will reach that elusive goal. There is power in the "Bottom Half" because that is where many of us live. That "Bottom Half" in part, can consist of us, our neighbors and our friends.

Notably, these are the people who help make all of our lives richer and more fulfilling. Many of the health care workers, retail clerks, cooks and waitresses fit in this category. These are people living on less than $56,811 per year. (This is the median income in Wisconsin from 2017 figures. It is lower than the national median income of just over $59K.) We couldn't really live without them because we don't have the skills or time to accomplish all those things for ourselves. "The Bottom Half" is full of important people...typically neighbors who are quite nice and patient as they work among us.

**While schools and pop psychology push us to be "our best,"** the truth is that not everyone will reach that elusive goal. **There is power in the "Bottom Half" because that is where many of us live.**

It is easy, though, to overlook this truth. Schools love to trumpet how many of their "Upper Half" students have won honors or awards. Their annual reports share how many are moving on to prestigious universities with eye-popping scholarships. Where are "Bottom Half" students mentioned? How are they served? How does the "Bottom Half" transition into worthwhile work? What happens to the "Bottom Half"?

Indeed, it is a wonderful accomplishment for such gifted students. Schools do deserve credit for helping them along the road to success. At the same time, it is probably true that even without schooling, these gifted students would have found success. There is much less direction, attention, support, and mentoring available for "Bottom Half" students. That leads to less hope for the future, less self-confidence, and less self-respect for these important young people.

What are we doing for the teens that do not find schooling a success story? Who advocates for their needs? How do they transition from High School to decent jobs?

The stereotypical "soccer mom" has the spunk and tenacity to fight for what they want for their kids. But the focus is on their kids and their friends. Who is going to fill the role of soccer moms for "Bottom Half" kids whose mom is working two jobs to keep food on the table or pay the rent. Most times these moms and parents don't have the time, vocabulary, confidence to advocate for their kids.

We need a better way to serve our under-served "Bottom Half" kids!

## TAKEAWAYS FOR DISCUSSION:

# CHAPTER 8

## School Visits – A Way to Open Our Eyes

I remember when I was growing up, my mother, a former teacher of the deaf, would invite my teacher over for tea. It was a "fall ritual" and boy, did I hate that because none of the other kids' mothers did that!

Worse than that, she would then proceed to tell me in detail how the tea time went. "Oh, your teacher is so nice. We had a great visit. You are very lucky to have a really good teacher." In my mind, I thought, "Oh, no! My goose is really cooked for another school year! My Mom and my teacher are going to be good friends!"

Home visits are a throwback to the days of the one-room rural schools where not only were teachers invited to the students' homes for dinner, but sometimes, they even lived in one of the student's houses for the whole school year.

As a young teacher, I made my first home visit (and my most memorable home visit) to Dave's house three or four weeks after school began in my first year of teaching eighth graders who were considered "slow learners" or "discipline problems" in Waukesha in 1964.

Most people considered Dave a real "failure." His shirt was always untucked. His hair long and greasy. He was just plain fat and flabby. He sat in the back of class with a sneer on his face. The other kids in the class seemed afraid to sit near him. He did nothing in class and no homework. He was a year older than the other students. The unwritten rule seemed to be that if the teacher left him alone, he did not bother anyone.

I called his house and made an appointment to visit his parents. It was hot the evening I came for the visit. The front door was open. I knocked and glanced inside. Dave's dad was laying on the couch in his boxers and an old-fashioned undershirt. He made no move, so I knocked again...louder. Then I said, "Mr. ---, I'm Dave's teacher and I made an appointment to see you."

"Yeah, what do you want?"

"May I come in?"

"Yeah."

Never during my short visit did he look at me. He just stared at the tv. Dave's mother was in the kitchen, but never came out to acknowledge me.

Dave was exactly like his dad. Dave couldn't read. By the middle of October, at age 15, Dave quit school and I never saw him again.

Strangely enough, the next year, I was surprised to find Dave's sister Sally in my class. She was my best student! She had quite an attitude. I quickly learned that she controlled the behavior of the entire class. She had more control of her peers than I did as teacher. She was a natural born matriarchal leader. We quickly developed an unspoken truce. I enjoyed my most successful class of my four year teaching career.

# CHAPTER 9

## Building a Child's "Education Team" – Parents, Teachers/Mentor, & Student

In my ideal world, each school would divide the number of teachers into the number of students, and each teacher would be the mentor of a child throughout the child's time at that school. This critical relationship asks teachers to respect and advocate for the child and to help the child feel comfortable not only with the teacher/mentor, but also in the school environment. This mentoring relationship will also help establish a positive relationship with the child's parents.

**Key aspects of building this relationship would include...**

1. An annual teacher home visit to establish and foster a working, respectful relationship in a non-confrontational atmosphere.
2. Teacher/mentor assumes the role of primary contact for the school when parental involvement is requested or needed either by the parent or the school.
3. Quarterly "values" grading score cards independently filled out by the child, as well as the teacher/mentor and the parents when possible. Then this would be the basis for a face-to-face review meeting of the three parties on a Quarterly basis (see chapters 41 through 43.)
4. The teacher/mentor would be easily accessible to their mentee students to help advise, protect, encourage and answer questions as needed.

This mentor relationship between teacher and child will occur quite naturally in many cases. However, it is critical that each student have a trusted and respected adult at their school to guide and advocate for them.

While in some school settings the schedule or culture may require annual changes in mentoring roles, the value of maintaining consistency cannot be over-stressed. There is great value in having these relationship develop and flourish over time.

Having long-term teacher/mentor and student relationship during elementary, middle school, and high school years would undoubtedly generate...

1. Strong, lifelong bonds that are rewarding both to teachers and students.
2. More stability in the "school world" for both teachers and students.
3. A more secure environment for educational success
4. Clearer focus on lifelong learning and values
5. A strong pathway for students to adult life

# CHAPTER 10

## Unheard Voices of the "Bottom Half"

I feel I should not have to write this to any American. There are so many voices that are unheard in the "Bottom Half" of our society. Those are the voices of parents looking for more for their children. They are the voices of children and teens who have little power to control their own destinies. These voices need to be heard and answered. They need hope. This proposal offers real hope.

In society, it is the innocent children that bear the toughest burdens. They need to fit into our society easily, innocently, and without malice toward them or pity for them. A child who is perceived as different bears the burden of being looked on by others who don't know him or her as having less to offer. Race, creed, color, handicapped, poorly parented, disadvantaged, unpopular: these qualities can easily become the burdens that destroy or limit a child's future.

These are the very children that should be given a high priority and the first opportunity to have their burdens lifted and to find success. Our schools, our communities, and our nation owe them an honest, unprejudiced opportunity to achieve "life, liberty, and the pursuit of happiness."

It is we and ultimately our society, in the end, whose lives are less rich and less meaningful. We ultimately must pay the price for our communities rejecting these innocent children and standing idly by when they are ravaged by their lot in life.

We do not begin to understand a child's burdens until we have visited their homes and in a small way walked in their shoes. Only in this way can we acquaint ourselves with their home environment and the challenges they face on a daily basis in those formative years of their lives.

It is important for schools to reach out to those whose voices are unheard and to learn of their relationships, hopes, and dreams for their children. The best way to reach them is in their homes. These visits could be made by teachers prior to the beginning of each school year. Or, this could be the work of a council of teens and parents who can begin family conversations and supply details of the Fox Valley Youth Apprenticeship Program in a simple brochure format.

*It is important for schools to reach out to those whose voices are unheard and to learn of their relationships, hopes, and dreams of their children.*

The purpose of the home meeting is to meet in a neutral, non-confrontational setting at a time that fits the family's schedule to explain and introduce the program. But, even more, the meeting is a chance to understand the family and how best to support the child. Home visits benefit not only the family being visited, but those doing the visiting. From my experience as a teacher and a parent, while receiving the information in a home setting is valuable, the true value of the home visit is in establishing friendly relationships for future communications with the parents and young people involved.

TAKEAWAYS FOR DISCUSSION:

# CHAPTER 11

## Behind Those "Pretty" School Pictures ...

Take a look at a school yearbook from any of our Fox Cities area high schools. The photo pages all look remarkably the same. They all look so happy. They all look poised for success. They all look ready to grasp their part of the American dream. But, as we all know, appearances can be deceiving.

Zach was not a bad kid. He was fun to be around. Maybe he wasn't a straight A student, but he was capable. For him it was the drugs and partying that caught him up. As the drugs he started experimenting with took more and more control of his life, his days and nights became a blur. He thought he could control "his problem." But the addiction finally won.

Zach's life ended far too soon. He made it longer than many. His obituary read:

***"Our precious Zach's story sounds far too common and familiar lately. On October 5, 2016 Zach died of an accidental heroin overdose. We share his story in the hope that it might save others from the incredible heartache we are experiencing."***

His heart was as big as his beard, and his smile and laugh would light up a room. There was never a question where Zach's heart was—he was real. He was kind. He was generous. He loved eggs benedict, prime rib, techno music, and glow sticks. He struggled with anxiety.

Zach loved spending weekends at the deer shack with family, snorkeling with his dad and soaking in the beauty of Door County. Zach took amazing photographs.

He was a big movie buff and could rehash the story line from every movie he ever saw ... Zach had a passion for riding motorcycles ... and loved his little dog Roo.

An addict is fighting an uphill battle. As loved ones, we intervene and do what we can to show tough love and help them out of their agony.

If you are struggling, or know someone who is - please do not wait until it is too late. At Zach's funeral, we will be reminded that the Lord asks us to lay down your burdens, lay down your shame, all who are broken, lift up your face. Oh wanderer, come home, you're not too far. So lay down your hurt, lay down your heart, and come to Him as you are.

In lieu of flowers, a memorial fund is being set up in Zach's memory ... do not be silent. Winnebago Crisis Center 920-233-7707 — Outagamie Crisis Center 920-722-7707."

# CHAPTER 12

## Maria's Story: Teen Pregnancy & Years of Paying the Price

There are so many stories. So many school pictures that belie the smiles on those student photos. Maria is one.

Maria is a waitress that I met at a local restaurant. Today Maria is on a path to success. It is easy to be happy for Maria today, she is back in school and on a track that will lead her to finding a successful nursing career. Maria's path, though, was a struggle. She's a single mom who as a young teen found herself pregnant and alone. Waitressing jobs make it a challenge for her to make ends meet for herself and her daughter, but she has persevered. Her teen years were lost as she spent those days raising her baby. Her success had to be postponed. While things are looking up now, Maria's path to successful adulthood was much harder than it needed to be because of her situation and mistakes she made early in life.

A while back, I spent some time in a local hospital. I was telling one of my nurses about this book and my theory about the dangers of idle time between 3:00 and 6:00 p.m. "Oh," she said, "That's me." She went on to relate that she had ended up getting pregnant one afternoon, after high school. For work, she landed a job as a CNA because she wanted to become a nurse. She worked nights and lived at home as she strove to gain her LPN license. In her own words, "I'm 36 years old now and got my RN four years ago. First, I did palliative care for dying patients.

I loved my work. I could see how I made a critical difference for my patients at the end of their lives."

This young lady made one mistake. Hers is a life of sacrifice for 20 years because of that mistake. How many lives could be positively affected by productively occupying those unsupervised hours of 3:00 - 6:00 p.m. during the school day?

# CHAPTER 13

## Help My Son ... or Is It Too Late?

Another acquaintance of mine is an unmarried immigrant who had been living with her partner through two pregnancies. She told me of her experiences raising her two, now young adult, children alone. Her daughter made it through school fine and is now studying for a professional degree. Her son, however, was diagnosed with ADHD.

The school insisted on sedating her son because of his "disruptive" classroom behavior. As a young mother, she went to the school leaders multiple times begging them to not require the sedative medication for him to attend school. The boy was not poorly behaved at home or in the community. The school's answer was always "no, he must take his medication." Today this young man can't hold a job and is largely uninterested in work. Instead, he drinks beginning each afternoon. Still sedated.

# CHAPTER 14

## Seven Nails – Aaron's Home Repair Business

If you had a home repair business, would you consider buying seven nails part of a successful day at work? Aaron is a young single dad. He was raised by his beloved grandmother who taught him as a teen to be handy with tools and home repair. He has been surviving in the Fox Cities as a home handyman. He is a bright, personable young man who works hard. Unfortunately, he has never been able to earn much money from the work he does. Why?

Being essentially self-taught, he has never been exposed to how others in his industry organize their time and materials for an eight-hour productive day of work. A typical day for Aaron means wasted time as he stops in the middle of his work day to do a quote or to run and get the materials he needs to finish the job he scheduled that day. One day he needed to interrupt his project and run to the hardware store to purchase the seven nails! Aaron is an example of an enterprising and hard-working young man who could have greatly benefited from on-the-job apprentice training and financial literacy help in high school.

## CHAPTER 15

# High School Basketball & Arrested Development

One day I was visiting with a friend who shared a disturbing story with me. It still bothers me. During a team practice at a local gym, there was a 1-on-1 basketball drill between two boys. One was black and the other was white. The competition was tough and both were playing hard. Things got heated and the two got into a scuffle. Adults jumped in to calm the situation. In the end, the white player was given a two-day suspension from the team. The black boy was arrested by the police, given a ticket, and now has a police record.

Now, I know that there are always two sides to an issue, two histories, or two sets of circumstances to be considered. I don't know all the "back story" to this situation, but I do know that those punishments were not equal. From what I understand, neither boy was a "discipline problem." Both were athletes. Clearly the consequences for each boy were different. One boy was disciplined by the coach; the other experienced his first entry on the police blotter. What does the future hold? What if there is a second fight? Would that be considered bullying? What might happen then?

If you were the black boy's parent, what advice would you give to your child? How would you go about trying to clear your son's name from the police records?

As I understand it, this was the story of a young man, a good basketball player, who had recently moved to town from another city in the Midwest. He had grown up in a bigger city, in a much different neighborhood, and a different school with a different culture. He was trying to find his niche in his new setting ... a hard challenge when it means breaking into the "club" of high school players who have been on the same teams since 4th grade and have been traveling together on an elite team honing their skills. Most kids who move into the new high school scene do not have the emotional resources to make this transition. With only five players on the floor at one time and only 6-8 boys playing major minutes, the stakes are high and parental politics are daunting.

What this boy needed was a mentor, not an encounter with the police. To take an illustration from the kitchen, the way the boys were treated was like having all the salt taken out of the black boy's meal and dumping it all on the other boy's food, effectively spoiling the food for everyone.

# CHAPTER 16

## Dyslexia & Other Learning Challenges

Dyslexia and other organic learning problems are handicaps that can stand in the way of many "Bottom Half" students and school success. As I understand it, roughly 20% of children, around the world and in America, wrestle with dyslexia reading problems. Students with these struggles deserve an "A for the Day" simply for showing up. They need special attention in our schools. I was shocked in my past two years of researching for this book when I discovered the effect of being able to read at only elementary school level has on teens, especially those in the "Bottom Half." With what is expected in school based on reading comprehension and skill, imagine how that increases exponentially for those who see the letters and words we can easily decipher as only a jumble of relatively meaningless scribbles.

Many dyslexic students are intelligent, but both they and their parents are frustrated with a system that often promotes them from grade to grade without addressing the root issue of their academic challenges. The embarrassment, the shame, and the anger can easily engulf these young lives and lead to disruptive behavior or worse. They are on a track for a very difficult life with a largely untreated or even diagnosed disability ... even in our excellent Fox Cities school systems. That is compounded if you are a minority student in the Fox Cities schools.

Sam has dyslexia and mild autism. Sam is now a junior in high school. He is a very nice teen with a fourth grade reading level because of his dyslexia. Outside of school he has never been in any trouble. Inside school he is treated as a "discipline problem." He acts out. He is angry and frustrated. Yet, he dreams of going to college. Sam's mother is spending thousands of dollars to try to help him overcome his dyslexia.

He is bright, but so discouraged by his situation. Standard schooling does not seem to hold the answer. Is there a way that restructuring the school setting could serve him and others with problems like him? Perhaps the Fox Cities Youth Apprenticeship Program could capitalize on his willing attitude and harness his work skills. A student with poor reading skills for whatever reason may be gifted in other ways ... perhaps being talented mechanically, creatively or being natural team leaders. Many are very good at multi-tasking projects because of their shortened attention span. As a former employer, I know there are many employment opportunities that can utilize these skills and talents despite a lack of reading skills. That would mean finding success instead of everyday frustration.

Areas of work that dylexic kids do well at are: machinist, graphic design, carpentry, landscape architecture, urban planning, photography, musician, acting and others. These creative teens would love to explore these careers.

To alleviate this troubling situation, the Children's Defense Fund recommends spending 40% more educating students with learning difficulties than what is spent on an average student. According to their statistics this would only amount to a cost difference per student of $4,400 (from $11,000 to $15,400 each). This investment in student success could pay big dividends.

# CHAPTER 17

## Kenny's Not Here Anymore

Kenny and his dad Ken were fixtures at the local Curling Club. Kenny was popular and accepted warmly by all club members. Together as father and son, they were pleasant and fun to be around. Kenny was a special needs student who was doing well in his classes. He was confident, cheerful, and his future looked limited but bright.

Kenny graduated from high school at age 19. He then went from a sheltered school environment to the work force. Kenny's dad found him a job at a friend's business doing janitorial work.

For a time, things went well, but after a year and a half Kenny was let go. Soon his dad found him another job. Sadly, this one did not work out either. Kenny's attitude and self-confidence were eroding. The school-to-work transition did not succeed.

After a year or so, Kenny's dad persuaded him to go to work at the local Goodwill store. Kenny was resistant. He felt he did not fit there. He was concerned about working with "handicapped" people. Still, he went and was hired. Kenny worked at Goodwill for a couple of years, but he was discouraged and unhappy. He made a mistake and was let go.

Friends from high school faded away. Except for his family, Kenny had few support systems in place. He felt lost and alone, frustrated and bitter about his situation in life. The next fifteen years were a series of job applications and rejections, sprinkled with a few short time jobs. At age 39, Kenny died.

Looking back at Kenny's story today, it seems like such a sad waste of a precious life. I can not help but wonder whether if the school-to-work sequence had been reversed, if the outcome would have been different. What if Kenny had been apprenticed for three years in High School to Goodwill or Valley Packaging for work and work environment training? They offer excellent programs. With apprenticeship and work training, could Kenny have then sought work through their placement services?

Could Kenny have been better prepared? Could he have had work that was more fulfilling to begin his career path? Would Kenny have been better acclimated in a reduced stress environment? Could he have gained important experience and the confidence to function successfully in the Fox Cities' work world?

It is clear that there is more that could have been done for Kenny in preparing him for the work force and life as an adult.

TAKEAWAYS FOR DISCUSSION:

# CHAPTER 18

## The Dangerous Time – 3:00 to 6:00 p.m.

You have heard nearly every political candidate expound on the "dangerous times in which we live." Build fear and it is easier to motivate action seems to be the theory. So let's take a look at some especially dangerous times that threaten the fabric of our society, culture, and communities.

Who can argue that our communities' children are the future of our society? It stands to reason. It needs no proof. The children of today are the workers, leaders, voters of tomorrow. Then consider that as many as 50 percent of our children are relatively drifting through their formative years and school life with little motivation. Couple that with the fact that many of these youngsters are substantially "on their own" from school dismissal to bedtime. The "free time" between 3:00 in the afternoon and dinner time (6:00-6:30 p.m.) is particularly troubling. You can be sure that unsupervised children are active, curious, hanging out together, and looking for "things" to do and limits to test. And once schools go on "summer vacation," the unsupervised time expands dramatically.

Temptations and experimentation pull our children in all kinds of directions during these hours each day. Peer pressure, the easy accessibility to illegal substances, the vile material they can expose themselves over the internet and their phones lead to growing delinquency, the breakdown of our community structure and legal trouble.

Beginning in the middle school years, as these young teens move into early adulthood, it is vital these precious individuals build life skills both so that they can enjoy a fulfilling, stable personal life and that our communities can benefit from their skills and talents at all levels as adults.

Recently Senator Cory Booker of New Jersey asserted that 1 out 4 of those imprisoned around the world are housed in United States prisons. Much of this is seen as the result of drug-related crimes. It is worth our time and energy to occupy our teens with productive work between the hours of 3:00 p.m. and 6:00 p.m. — a time when many "Bottom Half" teens are unsupervised.

According to Children's Defense Fund statistics released in 2016, plenty of Wisconsin teens could benefit from positive options during their unsupervised hours.

**TEENS (Age 10-17) ARRESTED IN 2016**

| Top 5 Highest Rates of Arrest | Percent | # Arrested | Population |
|---|---|---|---|
| Wisconsin | 9.291 | 56,054 | 5,788,708 |
| Wyoming | 7.050 | 4,144 | 585,501 |
| Nebraska | 6.075 | 12,293 | 1,907,116 |
| North Dakota | 5.788 | 3,982 | 757,952 |
| Colorado | 5.487 | 30,570 | 5,540,545 |
| **Lowest Rates of Arrest** | **Percent** | **# Arrested** | **Population** |
| Vermont | 1.152 | 686 | 624,594 |
| New York | 1.261 | 24,703 | 19,795,289 |
| Massachusetts | 1.386 | 9,816 | 6,811,779 |
| Kentucky | 1.418 | 6,496 | 4,434,974 |
| Michigan | 1.917 | 20,595 | 9,928,300 |
| US. Average | 3.084 | 1,024,600 | — |

How can Wisconsin be the state with the highest arrest rate for teens in the entire U.S. by over 2% and three times the national average? The positive alternative of apprenticeships may not be the whole answer, but successfully employing those 56,054 teens would have a major positive impact on that number of arrests and dramatically lower Wisconsin's expenditures for corrections! Plus, these alarming arrest rates for teens are indicative of why our state is in the upper half as a national leader in per capita adults in jail.

Wisconsin has the **highest rate of arrests for children ages 10-17 in the United States** and worse than that — **in most of the world as whole.**

## Each Day in America for All Children

| | |
|---|---|
| 2 | mothers die from complications of childbirth. |
| 4 | children are killed by abuse or neglect. |
| 7 | children or teens commit suicide. |
| 8 | children or teens are killed with a gun. |
| 22 | children or teens die from accidents. |
| 37 | children or teens are injured with a gun. |
| 45 | children or teens are injured or killed with a gun. |
| 64 | babies die before their first birthday. |
| 167 | children are arrested for violent crimes. |
| 311 | children are arrested for drug crimes. |
| 566 | babies are born to teen mothers. |
| 589 | public school students are corporally punished.* |
| 879 | babies are born with low birthweight. |
| 912 | babies are born into extreme poverty. |
| 1,414 | babies are born without health insurance. |
| 1,759 | babies are born into poverty. |
| 1,854 | children are confirmed as abused or neglected. |
| 2,805 | children are arrested. |
| 2,857 | high school students drop out.* |
| 4,388 | babies are born to unmarried mothers. |
| 12,816 | public school students are suspended.* |

*Based on 180 school days a year

## CHAPTER 19

# The Paths Teens Take

Typically, young people follow three paths to post-high school life: higher education, the military, and the workforce. Finding work is often a happenstance process. Many simply take the first job offered to them until a better opportunity comes along. Perhaps as we look back on our lives, that is what we see in our past.

Nonetheless, it is important to ask if that is the best way. That formative decade as a child matures to adulthood, let's say ages 13-23, are particularly unsuccessful for many kids. Drug and alcohol addictions, sexual experimentation, pornography, pregnancy, suicide, arrests, depression, abuse, bullying: all these are issues our teens struggle with today. Too many have little motivation and few successes to show for those teen years. There is little inclination to save money for future goals or needs and little modeling for the life skills needed to be successful in marriage and parenting.

Taking a close look at this troubling context, it is easy for schools to be satisfied with keeping teens docile and out of trouble. Simply reward families by passing students from grade to grade regardless of achievement. Let the "problems" move on and become someone else's concern next year. Keep the drop-out rates low and highlight the high-achieving students while drawing attention away from the fact that girls as young as 8th grade are becoming teen mothers at a much too early age and students are coming to school without food, decent clothing, or even following the basics of healthy hygiene.

Many people are surprised that Wisconsin has the highest rate of arrests for children ages 10-17 in the United States and worse than that, in most of the world as a whole. Precious lives are being wasted and shattered because it is easier to look away, gloss over, or ignore what is happening around us each day. This is not the fault of the schools, law enforcement, or the courts. Our laws reflect our community standards. (For the statistics, see Table 34 in the section from the Children's Defense Fund, page 186-187.)

We need to focus meaningful, effective, active attention on kids who are failing and falling through the cracks. They are not without talent, yet we continue to frustrate and alienate them. Our communities need to engage and develop their talents ... to help them find success. Note again that the Children's Defense Fund recommends spending 40% more per child for "Bottom Half" students.

Every child needs to be brought up with hope. They need to enter adulthood with curiosity and goals as well as reasonable expectation of success. Purpose, excitement, and opportunity fuel achievement. If our kids are failing in school and in life, who is to blame? An engaged apprenticeship will give teens hope.

The answer is not simple. The reasons vary from child to child, from family to family. The negative impacts of abuse, divorce, poverty, and bullying are all factors. In coming pages, this book will discuss not only the importance of understanding these negative impacts, but also dealing with these disparities in a way that respects each individual. Schools and social agencies are certainly part of the solution, but we need to take a close look at how our communities are "designed" and be willing to make changes that will make a difference in our society.

# CHAPTER 20

## Finding Solutions for "Bottom Half" Families

So, we see the many challenges and obstacles before our communities and especially before the "Bottom Half" of our communities. What is the solution? Where will we find answers? We do not have to look far and we do not have to dedicate vast amounts of money to address these needs.

For a long time, I debated about reprinting at least a section of the American Declaration of Independence in this book. It has been long time since most individuals have read this vital document from our country's history. The average citizen might remember that this is the document that includes the famous lines:

"We hold these truths to be self-evident: That all men are created equal; that they are endowed by their Creator with certain unalienable rights; that among these are life, liberty, and the pursuit of happiness."

In the lines following these oft-quoted lines are several key lines, not so well known, but that sound a warning to societies that do not adequately provide these rights to all their citizens. Those lines read: "That, to secure these rights, governments are instituted among men, deriving their just powers from the consent of the governed; that whenever any form of government becomes destructive of these ends, it is the right of the people to alter or to abolish it, and to institute a new government, laying its foundation on such principles, and organizing its powers in such form, as to them shall seem most likely to effect their safety and happiness."

That short phrase, "the consent of the governed," captures my attention. As I worked my way through creating this book, I wondered about how "the consent of the governed" applies to people who are marginalized or under-served in our communities. Do families trapped in poverty in our communities have the right to take a strong stand against the current status quo? Do "Bottom Half" students have the right to expect, or even demand, a better education or **brighter** future than what has been offered to them?

Really, have "Bottom Half" teens given their "consent of the governed" when it comes to the education system enforced on them? It seems to me that education today is more focused on the guidelines set by the local school boards, rules of the state departments of education, and Federal mandates. Are "Bottom Half" students being educated to step into promising futures as capable, experienced workers, or are they simply being asked to follow assigned curriculums to fulfill bureaucratic goals?

*Do "Bottom Half" students have the right to expect, or even demand, a better education or brighter future than what has been offered to them?*

To succeed in today's world, our teens need to be taught reading, math, and communication skills, as well as computer literacy. However, their education cannot stop there. The value of work needs to be a real part of the curriculum. I am suggesting a plan that provides students five hours per day in a paid work environment that prepares them to step into future employment. This is the kind of education that will motivate students, especially "Bottom Half Teens," and will provide experience and qualifications for roles in a broad range of employment opportunities available to them in our communities after high school graduation. Schooling needs to be more than an "academic" exercise for "Bottom Half Teens." It should ready them to step into desirable jobs and productive lives.

This is an important conversation our communities need to have, and it is the phrase "the consent of the governed" that makes this conversation so necessary. The words of this foundational document provide a welcome invitation that all parties need to meet and discuss this topic. The needs of all levels of society need to be met.

This principle works at every level in our American society. It is part of the fabric of our personal lives as well as our lives amidst society, government, school, work, and play. Effective implementation of the principle of the "consent of the governed" is how peace is brought into our world and our neighborhoods. **Effective implementation of the principle of the "consent of the governed" is how peace is brought into our world and our neighborhoods.**

**Less than half of poor children** are ready for school at **age 5** compared with **75 percent of their wealthier peers.**

- Children's Defense Fund

# CHAPTER 21

## Fox Cities – Let's Open Our Eyes and Be a Friend!

Many years ago Rotary President Bill Huntley shared an important speech entitled "Be a Friend." He quoted a 1943 presentation by Rotary founder Paul Harris who was asked the question: "Is everything all right with Rotary?" Harris' reply reiterated the question and provided a response and a challenge to its members.

"Is everything all right in Rotary? If so, God pity us. We are coming to the end of our day. No, thank God, everything is all wrong. There is probably no part of Rotary which cannot stand improvement. I like to think that the pioneering days of Rotary have just begun. There are just as many things to be done as there ever were. Rotary must continue to pioneer or be left in the rear of progress."

**Pause here and re-read the above paragraphs.**
**This time, substitute "education" in the place of "Rotary."**
**Is everything all right in EDUCATION?**

Huntley emphasized that the problems of illiteracy, homelessness, ill health, and poverty are not just local problems, they are worldwide ones. It is vital to discover the real needs of a community. Who's at fault for these crying needs is really immaterial. It is where help is coming from that matters. Our brothers and sisters, friends and neighbors are suffering and need our help. People, not problems, need to be our concern.

According to Huntley, each of us needs to ask ourselves these two questions:

1. How concerned are you to know and help YOUR COMMUNITY?
2. How concerned are you to know and help MY COMMUNITY?

This book seeks to begin with the community YOU are a part of and offers a template for change that can be transmitted to other communities around our state, our nation, and our world.

Huntley shared a quote from first lady Eleanor Roosevelt. "Where after all do human rights begin? In small places close to home, so close and so small that they cannot be seen on any map of the world. Yet they are in the world of the individual person: the neighborhood he lives in; the school or college he attends; the factory, farm, or office where he works. Such are the places where every man, woman, and child seeks equal justice, equal opportunity, equal dignity without discrimination. Unless these rights have meaning there, they have little meaning anywhere."

The challenge for each of us in Huntley's mind is to "Be a Friend." He reminds us that "A FRIEND is patient. A FRIEND is kind. A FRIEND is never jealous; never conceited; makes no demands; and never keeps a record. If you are a FRIEND, then you never give up. You never say 'That's enough.' A FRIEND is forever."

"These are stirring words. Words that stir FRIENDS into action. We know that the needs of our communities will never diminish. Chances are the challenges will increase. FRIENDS can sustain hope. FRIENDS can fulfill dreams. A FRIEND puts love into action in practical ways. That is our call to serve our communities."

Huntley's speech ended with a strong call to action. "So let us all give. Give our understanding. Give our talents. Give ourselves. To all those who wait. To all those who expect. To all those who need. BE A FRIEND!"

# CHAPTER 22

## Who Needs a Friend in the Fox Cities?

Consider for a moment: who is it that needs befriending in the Fox Cities communities? Certainly all of us need friends. At the same time, it stands to reason that while many of our Fox Cities citizens enjoy a stable and relatively happy lifestyle here, others are in particular need of finding that stability and happiness.

Look around you. Who are they? Those who wait on us with a smile everyday. Those who wait at bus stops for their transportation while we drive by. Those who have been laid off and are looking for work. The workers that staff our fast food stops, bars, restaurants, gas stations. Workers who have to settle for multiple part-time jobs because businesses don't want or can't afford to pay for full-time benefits. People with entry level jobs or unskilled laborers. Perhaps they are minorities or struggle with health or mental health issues. Maybe they are moms or dads who have been evicted and are struggling to make ends meet because of their poor credit history or who are being victimized by high interest loans.

So many are on the "edge" of life here in the Fox Cities. Young people kicked out of their homes. Teens with an early juvenile arrest record. Our ex-convicts trying to make a life for themselves. The list could go on. Older workers whose jobs have been eliminated and no longer have the skills or health to hold down the more lucrative jobs they once did. Workers with limited literacy. All these and more are "Bottom Half" issues.

Befriending those who struggle seems like an insurmountable obstacle. How can we take a meaningful step to make a difference? Many of these struggles begin early on in life for the "forgotten poor" or under-served in the Fox Cities.

# CHAPTER 23

## Starting with the Youth

I think the best answer is to start with our youth. There are many programs for preschool and elementary children which include Boys & Girls Clubs, YMCA, Scouts, churches and others. It is "Bottom Half Teens" that need effective, engaging community programs. I am struck by how vital it is to help teens navigate those troublesome years between ages 13 and 23. Getting them through those years without the traumatic effect of a life crisis that mars or interrupts their journey to maturity is key. It is a problem that is solvable.

It is solvable by replacing the idle, unproductive time in their daily schedule with time that successfully teaches them the skills to provide a meaningful future for themselves and their families by learning to work at a job they want.

I am proposing that education and business work together to create an environment in which is becomes normal and formative for our "Bottom Half" high school students to find excitement, motivation, and compensation though an effective, widespread apprentice program serving especially the "Bottom Half" of our high school age teens.

My only question is will community leaders recognize that each community is the only political agency that can humanely and cost effectively rescue their young lives trapped in a broken system.

If business can **utilize their best workers** to somewhat informally **mentor, befriend, or coach teens into developing self-confidence and good work habit** while finding direction, it is clear **everyone benefits.**

# CHAPTER 24

## Expanding Apprenticeship Options in Fox Cities Schools

Many schools already are organized for apprenticeships to happen for some students. It should not be difficult to expand this option to be the norm rather than the exception. Think of the benefits. We can greatly expand the options available to our students and offer our many businesses, nonprofits, and industry a source of future workers.

Some might argue that working with one high school class at a time is too slow. It will take 50 years for today's 15-year-olds to reach age 65! That is right. It will take 50 year to complete the cycle. Why is that a problem? The time to begin is now. The logical place to start is with this generation of young people before they enter the work force. Today's sophomores, juniors, and seniors need our help and our willingness to change a model that is not working. Look at history. Much can happen in a generation.

Consider the Civil War and all the changes that meant to society. Lincoln freeing the slaves, the bloodshed of American families fighting against their fellow countrymen, the President's assassination, the failure of President Andrew Johnson, Grant's ascension to the presidency. It was a time of turmoil and needed change. You could look at the Vietnam war in the same way. Great change. Great turmoil. The need for our society to move in new directions is strong. It is time to begin the process of change today.

If business can utilize their best workers to somewhat informally mentor, befriend, or coach teens into developing self-confidence and good work habits while finding direction, it is clear everyone benefits. Such work opportunities exist in both small and large employers and organizations. Healthcare, manufacturing, public service, professions, and nonprofits can all train young people in meaningful work that will prepare these students for success and good jobs in their future.

We have talked much about the "Bottom Half." I believe we need to spend as much time, energy and money on the "Bottom Half" of our sophomore, junior, and senior high school students as we do on our "Top Half" teens. All our young people deserve the opportunity to succeed in our society.

# CHAPTER 25

## Businesses & Employers Play a Key Role

As an employer who has years of experience in both large and small businesses, I found that my businesses depended on workers largely from "the bottom half" of their high school student bodies. I also found that the more interest we had in our workers, the more interest they had in their work effort and results. Often they told me that while they were capable or found modest success in high school, they were largely unmotivated in that setting.

Businesses can provide that motivation by working with these individual students in ways that capitalize on their excitement, curiosity and competitive spirit at the same time as the apprenticeship program affirms their value as a worthwhile individual.

If done well throughout the state, this apprenticeship program could save our state of Wisconsin billions of dollars. By diverting teens from issues that derail or traumatize their lives, the load on our criminal justice and mental health systems can be dramatically reduced. By any measure, it is clear that the problems of drug or alcohol abuse, bullying, violence, suicide, depression, jail, and early sexual activity exact a terrible toll on young lives. These traumas are not easily overcome and can haunt young lives for years and years.

The power of the apprenticeship program is its ability to add order, purpose, and structure to young lives in a relatively natural setting.

We tell students about life in the "real world." This is an opportunity for them to find a place to belong in "the real world." They can grow in self-confidence through measurable, visible "real world" achievements. In a meaningful way, they will be "earning" their way in life and discovering a path to maturity.

Maturity measures how we successfully handle issues. All of us have issues. Many stem from our upbringing or background. We all need to belong, to be a part of the society and culture around us, and to be accepted. We need to be important to others and to feel that what we do matters. This "school to work" plan offers a natural track for this to happen for 2,200 of our "Bottom Half" young people each year! Imagine the impact of 2,200 well-prepared workers entering the Fox Cities work force annually. In the ALICE report, (figure 40, appendix, page 169) the Work Force Development agency lists the future of changes due to the effect of technology of selected low and middle class jobs by 2025. It is a sobering prediction from Wisconsin government. We really need to organize education and business to prepare students to work through 2025 and beyond with work oriented training and the ability to change occupations.

The relationship-building aspect of mentorship is a major component of this proposal. Mentors are the people who shape our lives and serve as patterns for us. Mentors can be relatives, neighbors, coaches, fellow workers, supervisors at work or school. The "school to work" apprenticeship plan increases the chances of high school students having supportive mentors. In my mind, mentoring is typically not formal, but a natural outgrowth of being together and sharing similar goals and activities.

All of us fight battles from within. Then we make decisions and make the best of our decisions.

If anything, teens are making very tough decisions and they have less experience to help form a good choice. This is where a mentor fits in. Someone who is not paid, but available to answer a question, to talk to and listen when new life choices arise. A mentor is a friend.

# CHAPTER 26

## Mentoring: Another Key Aspect

Mentoring does not cost money, but does make life more meaningful and provides value for both the person being mentored and the mentor. In the work setting, this will occur naturally. No production time will be lost, but lives and productivity will be enhanced in the future as teens find a place where they matter and can make a difference. Successful work changes one's focus on life at any age. The mentors are not paid to mentor, but in the course of the day are asked to be supportive with the apprentices.

This being said, businesses have the obligation to provide healthy, desirable apprenticeship opportunities for our young people. These roles need to be ones that allow them to explore careers and offer a pathway to good jobs that have futures at occupations in which they want to work. Wages need to be at least $10 per hour or at scale if the students are more skilled.

Imagine for a moment that each Fox Cities high school participates. That would mean eventually 200 sophomores, juniors, and seniors from each school are employed in this "school to work" apprenticeship plan. With our eleven high schools, that would mean 6,600 Fox Cities teens exploring careers, building solid work habits, and being paid a meaningful wage for work well done. The result will be 2,200 work experienced, trained high school graduates will enter the Fox Cities work force each year.

Imagine how that could impact the work situation in the Fox Cities for years to come. With 2,200 apprenticeship positions available each year, 6,600 high schoolers would be exploring their future in our hospitals and health care facilities, construction, food service, automotive, small business, government, nonprofit, manufacturing, and service environments. With such a program in place, young people will be better qualified and businesses will be getting employees better able to step into new roles and be more productive.

Of course, the goal is not simply to benefit business. The goal is much larger. This is a quality of community issue. Earlier in this chapter, I referred to the importance of schools and business working together on this new model I am proposing.

# CHAPTER 27

## This is a Community Issue ...

Some might think that the issue of unmotivated students is simply a school concern, but a close look reveals it is not. The Fox Cities has quality schools. This issue transcends schools. It is a core issue that involves our Fox Cities families and communities.

I believe we need to address this as a coalition of families, schools, and business leaders. Our goals for our teens, especially those in the "Bottom Half," need to include providing all with...

**1. Hope for their future**

No child should emerge from their teen years without the confidence and desire to find success in life and to find worthwhile, fulfilling jobs that make a difference in the community.

**2. Resources to explore their future**

Children have a natural curiosity about what it means to be an adult. For "upper half" families, moms and dads typically have the opportunities and resources to share this vision with their little ones. The same is not always true with "Bottom Half" families. Nearly all children are born with the potential to succeed and make a difference in our communities. Programs offered by schools, local YMCAs, Boys & Girls Clubs help enormously to bridge that gap in the elementary years.

3. **Improved reading and math skills**

   67% of America's eighth grade students do not read at grade level. (See education charts in the Appendix, page 177-179, from Children's Defense Fund) Far too many young people today finish their formal education with poor reading skills. Reading comprehension is vital to future success in life and on the job. The same is true of math skills. These building blocks of literacy need to be the keystones of educational success. Without these in place, our children are immediately at a disadvantage. Why do our schools not vary the teaching methods for those students who are not successful in their current class curriculums?

4. **Improved financial literacy**

   Related to weak reading and math skills, families today seem more and more challenged to bring up children with an understanding of money and how it works in our lives. The importance of saving, understanding interest and the rule of 72, avoiding the pitfalls of credit, budgeting, and banking skills are often missing in the lives of young people. Part of the benefit of the apprenticeship program is that these young earners will have opportunities to learn firsthand about handling their own finances. They will need coaching. One possible condition for employment in the Fox Cities Youth Apprenticeship could be requiring the teens to participate in a savings/IRA contribution with employer match for retirement. Five years of saving $1000 per year could result in a retirement savings of $1,000,000 according to Warren Buffet's estimate of investing in Index funds. (See the chapter entitled "The Rule of 72.")

5. **Confidence of a place in their community**

   Life is more than individual successes. Psychologists tell us that America today is the loneliest generation ever. We hear of the dangers of peer pressure. Isn't giving in to peer pressure simply an indication that teens are looking for a way to fit in? All of us, young or old, need to be healthy mentally and emotionally. We need to be part of a larger community. On their path to adulthood, teens need to experience a sense of worth and the reassuring knowledge that they fit into our society or community.

In my estimation, we have to consciously create a realistic path to middle class living in the Fox Cities by building a work force that attracts employers who pay middle class pay scales. I suggest that our communities dedicate themselves to consistently focus on constructing that path for our 2200 high school age students. Having them qualified and well-trained creates a stable work force that will indeed attract employers who will pay middle class wages. The quality and depth of our young workers will be the very best reason for high-paying employers to locate to the Fox Cities. Educating our "Bottom Half" students for work success is a superior tool for desirable community development.

*I suggest that our communities dedicate themselves to consistently focus on constructing that path for our 2200 high school age students.*

A strong "School to Work" Apprenticeship program in the Fox Cities that brings together a partnership of schools and community will be the backbone for a solid future for "Bottom Half" students. From my experience, many of my best workers did not find success in the traditional high school setting. We hired them to work and coached them to learn what it meant to be a productive worker and build solid living skills.

# TAKEAWAYS FOR DISCUSSION:

# CHAPTER 28

## Fox Cities Action Plan for Apprenticeships

### STEP 1: Involving Our Schools

You might say that creating a program for 6600 kids is unmanageable and unrealistic for both schools and employers.

No. If we set annual participation limits by adding only 25 kids at each grade level per high school per year, and if kids are excited about the jobs being offered, we can grow to 6600 participants in ten years. Since Apprentice programs are already operating in our schools, we can begin with 25 sophomores per high school and increase another 25 each year until we reach 200 in each class for all eleven high schools. In order to create excitement and competitiveness, the apprenticeship program should have more kids applying for apprenticeships than we have available.

| School Year | # of High Schools | Grade 10 | Grade 11 | Grade 12 | Total |
|---|---|---|---|---|---|
| 2018-19 | 11 | 25 | 0 | 0 | 275 |
| 2019-20 | 11 | 50 | 25 | 0 | 825 |
| 2020-21 | 11 | 75 | 50 | 25 | 1650 |
| 2021-22 | 11 | 100 | 75 | 50 | 2475 |
| 2022-23 | 11 | 125 | 100 | 75 | 3300 |
| 2023-24 | 11 | 150 | 125 | 100 | 4125 |
| 2024-25 | 11 | 175 | 150 | 125 | 4950 |
| 2025-26 | 11 | 200 | 175 | 150 | 5775 |
| 2026-27 | 11 | 200 | 200 | 175 | 6300 |
| 2027-28 | 11 | 200 | 200 | 200 | 6600 |

NOTE: It is important for each school to be proportionately sized according to enrollment each year. The number of 200 students per year is an example. Since school sizes vary, the number of participants will actually be proportioned according to student population and student needs.

1. Each school can develop a diversity of jobs.
2. "Bottom Half" students who need mentoring and opportunities need to receive top priority.
3. Kids apply competitively for jobs that are developed and can hopefully continue from year to year. Employers, parents, and schools benefit from a limited supply of opportunities, and kids apply to offer employers a choice of prospects.

# CHAPTER 29

## Fox Cities Action Plan for Apprenticeships

### STEP 2: Organizational Structure

Organization is vital to accomplishing this apprenticeship program. The key would be to create a structure in each high school that focuses on consensus building and working collaboratively.

I propose an Apprenticeship Task Force of 110 members that represents 10 people at each of the eleven Fox Cities high school. At each high school the Task Force might be comprised of:

- 1 school administrator in charge of apprenticeship programs
- 2 employer representatives (one representing a larger employer and one representing a small or medium sized employer, but both representing a range of possible jobs for future employees.)
- 1 community nonprofit representative
- 2 parents of "Bottom Half" students
- 4 "Bottom Half" students

The purpose for this structure is to actively engage the key players involved in this apprenticeship program: education, local business leaders, and "Bottom Half" families and students. This would be the best way to ensure the program serves the needs of teens and young adults in preparing them for success in the world of work and beyond. The two parents from "Bottom Half families" at each school are key so that the schools and business representatives better understand the challenges that "Bottom Half" families face on a daily basis. The students will contribute more and learn more than anyone else if this structure is run correctly.

One of the key tasks of the High School Task Force is to manage the job application process. By making the process clear, understandable, and straightforward, this will add an "attractiveness" to "Bottom Half" families as they see jobs being offered that hold a future for the apprentices who are hired. Employers need to assist by providing job descriptions that are equally clear, understandable, and straightforward so that students know what they are applying for. These job descriptions need to highlight the opportunities for future advancement, benefits, and pay ranges, not just at the present time, but even 10-20 years into the future, to emphasize the value of this career path and its potential.

Students will need to review the job descriptions and then apply for those they are interested in. Employers will then need to review the applications and choose the apprentices who will best suit their needs. This needs to begin in June and may take all summer for some students.

The goal and the reality is that this is a real-life experience. Competition creates value for the teen applicants. The application process offers them valuable experience at the job hunting process. Many people in the "Bottom Half" have varying degrees of difficulty managing job applications. Perhaps they have reading difficulties, ADHD, dyslexia, or other learning disabilities.

Schools, parents, students, and employers need to learn how to manage this application and hiring process. Effective presentation of the jobs, understanding the expectations and the benefits offered with being hired for a position, coupled with the expectation and satisfaction of working for real wages (money that will actually go in their pockets) is an exciting opportunity.

Additionally, managing the day-to-day issues and challenges of transportation to and from work, meals, attendance, and work deportment will offer another learning curve. Car pooling or use of public transportation needs to be organized for each student. This is a role the Task Force can fill. School buses and even good, "old-fashioned" walking or biking are possibilities, especially if jobs can be located within a mile or two of the participating schools.

In my estimation each High School Task Force should meet at least on a monthly basis in the beginning to start this program on a firm foundation. High schools that already have strong apprenticeship programs would most likely have an initial advantage as they look at implementing this plan since they may already have leaders in place to make this happen sooner versus later. Perhaps those schools can provide leadership to our other local high schools who do not currently have much of an apprenticeship program.

It would also be important to host quarterly meetings of the entire Fox Cities Apprenticeship Task Force. These could be hosted at the high schools involved or at community employers with appropriate facilities. Breaking up the sessions so that students can meet with other students, business leaders with other business leaders, educators and their counterparts, as well as parents with other parents, would be helpful and desirable. Leaders could use this time to share challenges and successes as well as to look to future ways to improve their program. If hosted at community employers, it would also be an opportunity to observe facilities and partnerships.

Poor children are more likely to have **poor academic achievement, drop out of high school** and later become **unemployed, experience economic hardship** and be involved in the **criminal justice system.**

- Children's Defense Fund

# CHAPTER 30

## Fox Cities Action Plan for Apprenticeships

### STEP 3: Funding the Plan

My firm belief is that this apprenticeship plan should require no new taxes or major private funding. Also no education jobs should be lost.

It would require thinking about and structuring the school day in a little different way. However, since some high schools are already running apprenticeship programs, it is not a radical change in concept, simply an expansion of those efforts to meet the needs of more "Bottom Half" students and their families.

In this Fox Cities Apprenticeship Plan, high school students involved in the program would have a schedule which has them in school for their education requirements five hours per day. Following their "education block" of time, students would then be released to attend their five hour "apprenticeship" block of time where they would report to work. One half would work morning hours (7:00 a.m.-12 noon) and the other half would work afternoon hours (1:00-6:00 pm). It also may be practical to have a 4:00-9:00 pm shift.

In the high schools, having students attend for five hours each day should "free up" some school staff members to fill important roles in the running of this program, especially as it expands in size.

I would foresee needs for ...

1. A full-time liaison
2. A job developer and coach for employers
3. A support staff person or manager

For employers involved in the Fox Cities Apprenticeship Plan, once the program is properly set up, should they not need to spend more time on training apprentices than they would any other new employee. In fact, if the job placement can be kept competitive for the students, these young adults, given a chance to earn their own way at a job they find fulfilling, should yield surprisingly good results.

*In this Fox Cities Apprenticeship Plan, high school students involved in the program would have a schedule which has them in school for their education requirements five hours per day.*

Will there be struggles? Yes, some of these young men and women will be struggling. Employers can add purpose, achievement, and a path out of poverty for them. That may take additional patience and coaching. For employers, it may also be exceptionally rewarding! These are alternate paths for our youth. Making them as constructive as possible, and not destructive, benefits all involved ... a fine line to build lives.

Employers who treat their new employees right will be a corporate friend in their community. As such, they should prepare to make room for fresh faces, fresh enthusiasm, and fresh opportunity. Teens will respond to having new "friends" in their "Bottom Half" world, friends who provide honest, real life opportunities.

# CHAPTER 31

## Fox Cities Action Plan for Apprenticeships

### STEP 4: Action Planning

Each teen is important. All of us have heard about teens and families that "fall through the cracks." Take a close look at the world our "Bottom Half" families live in, even here in the Fox Cities.

We have too many kids that drop out, that are passed through school unable to read beyond an elementary level, and simply not engaged in career growth and exploration.

The failure of the Fox Cities community to be effective with many disadvantaged and poorly motivated teens, despite our present best efforts, needs to be addressed. We need to focus on kids who are failing, who don't have the advantages of solid mentors or stable homes, or even a voice in their own future.

Failure is very expensive!

In Wisconsin, the corrections system has a larger budget than our educational system! Mental health and substance abuse issues need to be reduced. We need all of our teens, not just the highly motivated or talented ones, to become productive self-sufficient adults.

This action plan lays out a clear path to meeting this vital need in the Fox Cities. It is not only to engage and focus on students who are disadvantaged and lacking equal opportunity, but it also offers them successful employment during the dangerous hours each day from 3:00 to 6:00 pm and in the summer when they are often unsupervised and on their own.

Consider the positives...

The Fox Cities Apprenticeship Plan provides a way to help young people deal with many of the pressures of today's society and culture. By offering them a worthwhile alternative, it could lead to:

- less smoking addictions
- less substance abuse
- less sexual experimentation and teen pregnancies
- reduced depression/suicide issues
- reduced contact with the criminal justice system
- improved self-image
- improved self-confidence
- less addiction to social meida, the internet and video games
- productive work relacing the time spent on the virtual world attractions

Additionally, it will equip students to be better trained employees who are conversant with computers, robots, and other modern technologies. It will also mean young adults who will develop a stronger work ethic, a better understanding of working relationships, improved money management skills, and are more mature and prepared for successful family life.

# CHAPTER 32

## Fox Cities Action Plan for Apprenticeships

### STEP 5: After High School – Transitioning to Work & Preparing for Life

One of the most difficult aspects of graduating from high school for "Bottom Half" teens is obtaining a worthwhile job. For the majority, they have little idea what they want to do in life. They are frustrated because employers want experience and skills. But where does an 18-year-old get experience? That means what is typically available to them is entry level positions or no skill jobs that lead nowhere.

One of my young friends is struggling with this very problem. He is a bright young man seeking responsibility, but not quite sure what he wants to do. He was raised well and is in the top 25% of the "Bottom Half" group. This friend is well-behaved, adjusted, has a great attitude toward work, and never causes a problem. How does he "break through" the process of finding a job that matters?

He tells me that many of his friends are not interested in attending college and could not get classes that prepare them to develop skills for the types of jobs that interest them that include carpentry, mechanical, or factory skills. He is now 20 years old and nothing outside of low skill jobs is available to him.

The worst of this situation is that every employer in our area needs his attitude, his potential, his morals, values and honest energy. The Fox Valley Action Plan for Apprenticeships addresses this problem. Clearly the "old ways" are not working. For "Bottom Half" young adults like my friend, his prospects are not welcoming or engaging. He realizes that he is "frittering away" some of the best years of his life.

Clearly, our communities need to develop a process to productively bring young people through their school years into their adult years successfully. Recently the new verb "adulting" has made it into the American vocabulary. The context is that "adulting" is difficult or that "I really don't feel like adulting today." There is much concern that university level studying is giving young adults even more reason to avoid graduation and assuming their role of responsibility in society today.

Perhaps instead of the emphasis on how many students graduate from high school and move on to college, it is time to shift the focus. Why do we not aim to shift the emphasis not to how many teens move on to college, but on how many have found their way to meaningful success in the work world? And maybe, if they start out with meaningful work, they will choose a specific college curriculum that will advance them in their working career.

*Clearly, our communities need to develop a process to productively bring young people through their school years into their adult years successfully.*

A number of area high schools have already taken steps in developing apprenticeships. The Fox Cities Chamber has a full-time staff person working with parents, educators, and employers.

Menasha has a strong summer school program that not only engages students with remedial programs, but also provides courses that allow students to explore nature, literature art, and other interests or hobbies. While designed more for K-8 students, wouldn't it be interesting to extend this model for high school students in the summer?

Extending creative learning for another six to eight weeks in the summer and coupling that learning with five to seven hours of work five days per week will go a long way to creating a "summer vacation" that has positive, lasting results instead of idle, undirected, unsupervised time. Even with the additional "schooling," this would leave four to six weeks of vacation time for students.

It is also important that our local post-high schools continue to step up to the challenge of serving the "Bottom Half" students. This concept is vital for the transition of "Bottom Half" students to rise above the difficulties of life they experienced in elementary, middle school, and high school. For many it is the key for them to break out of the cycle of poverty.

If, after high school, employers can commit to providing two years of tuition assistance for their "Bottom Half" students at either the local technical college or university center, the door can be opened to better utilize the idle time and to better develop their talents educationally post high school. This transition time is a vital key to future success.

Undoubtedly, some post-high school students will need to choose full-time employment and part-time education. Others will be able to make the schedule of part-time work and continued schooling for five hours per day part of their routine. These "two years" mentioned in the paragraph above may end up lasting anywhere from two to four years depending on the student's needs and desires. With employers and the two colleges enhancing their partnerships to support the students in this way, the chances of successful transitions into adult lives is dramatically increased.

On the other hand, **there are multiple methods to teach both reading and math in the elementary schools and beyond.** Why don't we have teachers trained in multiple methods to **reach the 2/3rds of students that struggle reaching grade level skills?**

# CHAPTER 33

## The Role of Teachers

Teachers are great people. They are talented at managing the classroom, discipline and teaching academics. But teachers cannot teach work. That is not to say they do not work. Anyone who has taught (and there are many teachers and former teachers in our population) knows educators work hard and love the students they teach.

Teachers do not teach work. Happily, our community employers do teach work. This includes many aspects of what it means to work, examples which are habits, standards, idiosyncrasies, on-the-job knowledge about products, techniques and methods plus communication skills about working and its processes.

Hospitals, factories, service industries, nonprofits, government, and even educators know how to teach, guide, develop, nurture, coach, mentor and develop work in their own areas of enterprise.

It is unfair to expect teachers to teach all these variable skills and aspects of work outside of the atmosphere of work. Educators are already expected to teach too much outside of academics and pure knowledge.

On the other hand, there are multiple methods to teach both reading and math in the elementary schools and beyond. Why don't we have teachers trained in multiple methods to reach the 2/3rds of students that struggle reaching grade level skills?

Every dictionary entry starts with the word printed in bold spelled correctly and with syllabication. Immediately following is the word spelled phonetically.

Why is this important in Webster's Collegiate Dictionary when phonics are generally discarded by schools?

Unbelievably, 67% of American 8th graders DO NOT READ AT GRADE LEVEL and math is close behind.

Citizens must rally together and dictate change.

# CHAPTER 34

## Technology and Its Impact on the Future of "Bottom Half Teen" Jobs

One of the startling statistics in the back of this book is the percent of jobs in selective categories that will be either eliminated. or significantly changed by technology. Developed by the Wisconsin Department of Workforce Development some of our largest job classifications are changed by 70, 80 and even 90 plus percent.(see pages 170-172).

We are all ready seeing the technology impacts in our daily lives. Go to McDonald's and order a soda. Go to the grocery store and check yourself out. Go to the Amazon prototype store here you don't even need a cash register. Go to Phoenix and take a ride in a driverless car. Who knows how fast these changes will be a normal part of our lives. What will be next?

Are our high schools preparing students to manage for these major changes students will face in the first 10 years in their careers? Do we even teach computers and coding in high school? Why not? One of Ryan Long`s power point slides explains clearly how a person's level of education has a disproportionately large effect on those less educated, i.e. "The Bottom Half."

These are the skills and programs we need teach, for work today:

**Lower elementary:** Scratch Jr.
**Upper elementary:** Scratch
**Freshmen:** Microsoft
**Sophomores:** Macintosh
**1st semester Juniors:** SQL
**2nd semester Junior:** JavaScript
**1st semester Seniors:** PHP
**2nd semester Seniors:** Tutorial Project

If we challenge kids on computers they will get excited. Bottom Half Teens will too! Graduates with these skills are needed by employers.

Real computer skills will make teens more desirable during their Apprenticeships.

I think apprenticeships can do that for the majority of the Bottom Half Teens. Perhaps one Fox Valley Technical College style class each year, for the four years of high school, could be very significant. I don't mean to ignore the top half, but I am focusing on teens in the Bottom Half.

Future technology based education beyond high school for two to four years will be helpful for a lifetime of technology at work and at home. Business, industry and services need to work with school boards and high schools at the local level as they have with the local technical colleges to transition teens from school to work in a technical world.

Unfortunately, India, China, Indonesia and Vietnam are not sleeping. The real trick in America will be to constructively engage Bottom Half Teens to want to be adept with technology.

Apprenticeships!
Apprenticeships!
Apprenticeships!

# CHAPTER 35

## Key Partners:
Fox Valley Technical College (FVTC)

For many years, FVTC has filled a vital role in our communities in assisting high school graduates in transitioning to the adult world of work. This work is even more vital today and many teens seem to be struggling to make this move. The great news is that FVTC continues to do more of what they already do so well.

**The role of Fox Valley Technical College remains . . .**

1. to continue to partner with high schools in providing quality, challenging, in-depth education opportunities to introduce graduates to the work world. As area high schools move to incorporate more curriculum options for "Bottom Half" students, FVTC becomes the perfect partner to provide guidance and to help the high schools integrate their course offerings with FVTC programs. In brief, this means that many of the 2200 participants in the Fox Cities Apprenticeship Program will be exploring the ever-evolving levels of technical education.

2. to present 18- and 19-year-olds with the opportunity to complete their two-year Associates Degrees and be well prepared to enter the work force while continuing to work on advanced apprenticeship roles.

3. to extend additional opportunities to these young adults through their four-year course programs and prepare their students for the wide variety of vocations they offer including engineering, computer science, health care, nursing, nutrition, public safety, and more.

Industry would be wise to consider scholarships for student apprentices who would be willing to challenge themselves with the full program of schooling that would take them into their early 20's. In this way, industry will be developing and stabilizing an attractive, qualified, long-term workforce. If done well, these employers will be gaining long-term appreciative employees.

# CHAPTER 36

## Key Partners:
UW-Oshkosh Fox Valley Center

The role of the UW-Oshkosh Fox Valley Center could be independent of or work in conjunction with Fox Valley Technical College to enable "Bottom Half" teens to obtain two-year or four-year degrees in the students' area of interest.

The UW-Oshkosh Fox Valley Center is an excellent academic college which can now offer evolving STEM degrees with both Bachelor of Science and Bachelor of Arts degrees. Here again UW-Oshkosh Fox Valley Center students should be able to participate and work in the advanced apprenticeship programs proposed in this book.

This effort to formalize advanced apprenticeships will enhance our communities' commitment to assist "Bottom Half" teens with effective work preparation from ages 13-23. Young people who have found success through age 23 without major flaws on their resumes are much more likely to achieve productive working and family lives to age 65.

This proposed extended apprenticeship program can limit the pain and suffering in young lives from negative behaviors simply by being engaged in positive work experiences.

# CHAPTER 37

## Who Leads This Effort?

Schools need to be actively engaged in the development of this concept that means revamping school days for "Bottom Half" students into a full day of education and apprenticeship activities.

Remember, this is a larger community issue. We need to evaluate the speed and process of developing work opportunities. We need parent engagement. And, most important, our young people need to be big part of the process. They will be our best sales people to their class mates.

Involving community nonprofits like the United Way, the Community Foundation, the Boys and Girls Clubs, the YMCA, Leaven, Habitat for Humanity, or Goodwill is also important since they bring better understanding of the challenges of "Bottom Half" families and students to the planning process.

The earlier suggestion of the Fox Cities Apprenticeship Task Force at each of our eleven Fox Cities high schools is certainly part of answering the leadership question.

*Remember, this is a larger community issue. We need to evaluate the speed and process of developing work opportunities.*

Employers and leaders from business and the non-profit community need to address the issues of job creation, quality of process, and carefully monitoring and opening permanent long-term employment in jobs where employee career growth and development is a focus.

The Fox Cities needs to address these critical needs now. We need to start increasing the apprenticeships this year, 2019-2020. We can grow by building on the apprenticeships already in existence. We need leaders to step up, use this book as the beginning of an action plan, and create a solid future for Fox Cities teens in the "Bottom Half."

# CHAPTER 38

## Another Community Partner:
Chamber of Commerce

Another important partner in establishing and empowering the Fox Cities Youth Apprenticeship Program are the local Chambers of Commerce. The Fox Cities Chamber is already an active partner of the existing apprenticeship programs in the Fox Cities high schools. These organizations are usually thought of as a collection of business, industry, and service companies operating in a community to protect and preserve their broader business climate and growth opportunities. The focus of developing a competent employment base is an effort that certainly appeals to their members.

This entire project is meant to be driven by the community for the benefit of the community. While this problem is a national one, and while if enough communities pick up this concept it could have a national effect, each effort needs to be a local one. The reason is because we must assist "Bottom Half" teens and families need to be organized locally by those who live in and understand each high school's local struggles and challenges.

Chambers of Commerce can play an important role in this effort. They are a natural and less political coordinator of the local youth apprenticeship effort. They are a strong voice and one that can organize a lobbying effort on the state level to support legislation which favors movement toward this end.

As a former Chamber of Commerce executive for seven years, I believe the chamber can be help our communities build a structure for this program so that it is operating on a neutral, as much as possible, playing field where special interests and traditional power structures can be led to adopt this constructive structural change. The base goals will best be met if we include the poor and minorities of "Bottom Half" families in the decision making process.

Developing a community dialog and adding instruction beginning as early as preschool with components of learning effective communication skills, people skills, and work habits is vital and a path for future success as an adult.

Ultimately, this book is about problems that affect our entire community and offers an approach to solve these problems by the community, THE FOX CITIES COMMUNITY.

## TAKEAWAYS FOR DISCUSSION:

# CHAPTER 39

## Where are Today's Farm Kids?

When I was an employer, the first person I wanted to hire was a "farm kid." Why? Farm kids knew how to work. They worked hard and were willing to do the tough jobs. You could always count on farm kids. Parents set the example. Farm kids learn how to depend on themselves. Also, they see the fruits of their labor every day.

We can take a lesson from this today. That is what this book is about. The path out of poverty is to learn how to work well.

Of course, there are less and less farm kids in our American world or in the Fox Cities. How do we find farm kids where there aren't many. I think we need to train our children to be today's "farm kids."

I have a friend who is an excellent tradesman. Talking to him about this book, he volunteered that he would "just love to work with a teen and teach him my trade. I would have him work alongside me. No bullshit, just work. The kid would have to keep up ... I mean I would tough on him, but fair and kind. I would teach him so much he would become the best in the Fox Cities and he would be able to take his skills anywhere he wanted."

I hope my friend gets that opportunity and I hope one or more of our Fox Cities students get the chance to work with him and find success. This tradesman would be an exceptional match for a special kid who needs a chance to earn his way into a solid profession. I know this man's own children. The “Bottom Half” teen who is fortunate enough to be matched with him will find a great mentor and coach.

So many “Bottom Half” teens are dealing with mental, physical or emotional abuse issues. They have had poor or no adult role models to follow with little coaching or mentoring by caring individuals. Yet, these kids who may be the most difficult to employ are the ones who need the opportunity the most. Left to themselves, these are the kids who will most likely become the greatest burden to society.

Sadly as they lose themselves, they often bring others with them including their family and friends. Police records, professional interventions, and difficult times loom ahead for those we allow to fall through the cracks. Being a friend to our “Bottom Half” teens means extending ourselves to the “least of us” on a daily basis to make a difference in their lives.

# CHAPTER 40:

## Not the European Model – This is America!

Some might argue that this apprenticeship proposal is just a warmed over version of the European education model. Actually, there is a major difference between the two.

In Europe, the education system has two tracks: university track and the skilled labor track. Students must pass a rigorous test to enter the university level of study. This proposal offers "Bottom Half" students of the Fox Cities the opportunity for either skilled or academic education and a structure which supports the chance to choose one and then, later, the other based on student initiative and desire.

This is significant.

The "American Dream" has always been that with hard work, our citizens have the ability to find success on their terms and to work to achieve their dreams and desires. This apprenticeship proposal offers a concrete pathway for "Bottom Half" high school students to earn success through hard work and initiative. Their education choices will determine their work choices. It will not be mandated by tests that force them into required tracks of study.

This **apprenticeship proposal** allows that this might be a **better way to grade students** than the typical **A - B - C - D - F scale** that education has **become so attached to.**

# CHAPTER 41

## What's the Grading Scale?

Agree or Disagree: Work is Pass or Fail. Or, more precisely "Pass or You're Fired."

As a former teacher, I would assert that grades are inherently unfair for students. You have the A students with photographic memories who can earn an A with little to no work, but are not well adjusted socially. While you have C students who can work as hard as is physically possible and seem to never get higher grades. In terms of effort, shouldn't those C students be getting the A's and this A student be graded lower. This apprenticeship proposal allows that there might be a better way to grade students than the typical A - B - C - D - F scale.

Adopting some form of kaizen or "lean" improvement practice in which employees meet to accomplish productivity and process improvement would be much more valuable and realistic than a traditional school grading scale. This process would allow students to learn the why and the how as well as the "I can," "I want to," and "I care" to become a productive and committed employee. Teens need positive, value-based and real-world education.

I found such a value-based evaluation format very successful when I conducted annual reviews in my own company. Employees evaluated themselves at the same time as I filled out an evaluation on them. Then we exchanged our forms to review and then to discuss together.

Generally, the employees were much tougher on themselves than I was. It was a way for me to positively work to modify behaviors and values. My goal was to create a positive atmosphere on our plant floor.

The analysis was pretty simple. I asked the employees about how they felt they were doing in the areas of effort, perseverance, diligence, knowledge of their job, and relationships with other workers. Other questions I asked included...

1) What would help you be neater and more organized in your work?

2) Where do you need help?

3) How could we make work better?

4) How can we increase production?

5) How can we better serve our customers?

Such assessments were sometimes oral and sometimes written. I used this method of evaluation with everyone in the company for several years. After that, I used it only with new employees or employees who seemed to be struggling in being effective at their job.

The advantage is that the process is personal and brought us together as fellow workers. I found it required my attention to detail about these valuable members of our company.

I absolutely believe this would be a much better evaluation system for our Fox Cities schools to adopt. Letter grades do not truly help students and they certainly do not help all students equally or fairly. A's, B's and C's don't motivate any except the honor students. Even then, they are false indicators of student character and self-image. National test like the ACT or SAT are far better indicators of educational skill achievement.

I find little value in teachers giving students D's or F's or even C's. Middle school and high school students need to set their own realistic standards and evaluate themselves (with teacher help) on how well they are moving toward success on those standards. This could also be an important way to make parent-teacher conferences meaningful and valuable to parents. In this way, parents would be involved in important conversations about the evaluation of their child's success in learning.

# CHAPTER 42

## The Values Growth Chart© Evaluation Scale

**Value Growth Chart Directions:**

The Values Growth Chart is meant to be a starting point for each High School, if not community, to develop their unique community values. The Values Growth Chart is to be filled out by each student, their parent(s), teacher and/or mentor.

1. **Student:** Complete the evaluation chart by marking the circle across from each value where **YOU** feel **YOU** display that value most accurately.
2. **Parent(s), teacher and/or mentor:** Complete the evaluation chart by marking the circle across from each value where **YOU** feel the **STUDENT** displays that value most accurately.
3. **Student, parent(s), teacher and/or mentor:** Under each value is a comment section. When helpful, use that open space to clarify your value rating.
4. The last page should be a summary of the teams recommendations on areas to work on based upon the individuals value growth plan.
5. It is recommended that The Values Growth Chart is to be repeated three times throughout the year: beginning, middle and end. Meet as a team to discuss how the student is doing. From year to year, note how the value is trending and chart a path forward.

Students Name: ____________________________ Grade Level: _____________

Evaluaters Name: ___________________________

Relationship to Student: ***(circle one)*** Student Parent Teacher Mentor

| | ALWAYS | OFTEN | SELDOM | RARELY |
|---|---|---|---|---|
| **Fair** | ❍ | ❍ | ❍ | ❍ |
| *Comment:* | | | | |
| **Friendly** | ❍ | ❍ | ❍ | ❍ |
| *Comment:* | | | | |
| **Neighborly** | ❍ | ❍ | ❍ | ❍ |
| *Comment:* | | | | |
| **Angry** | ❍ | ❍ | ❍ | ❍ |
| *Comment:* | | | | |
| **Shares** | ❍ | ❍ | ❍ | ❍ |
| *Comment:* | | | | |
| **Trusted** | ❍ | ❍ | ❍ | ❍ |
| *Comment:* | | | | |
| **Polite** | ❍ | ❍ | ❍ | ❍ |
| *Comment:* | | | | |
| **Included** | ❍ | ❍ | ❍ | ❍ |
| *Comment:* | | | | |
| **Neat** | ❍ | ❍ | ❍ | ❍ |
| *Comment:* | | | | |
| **Clean** | ❍ | ❍ | ❍ | ❍ |
| *Comment:* | | | | |
| **Hurtful** | ❍ | ❍ | ❍ | ❍ |
| *Comment:* | | | | |
| **Listens** | ❍ | ❍ | ❍ | ❍ |
| *Comment:* | | | | |
| **Well Behaved** | ❍ | ❍ | ❍ | ❍ |
| *Comment:* | | | | |
| **Appearance** | ❍ | ❍ | ❍ | ❍ |
| *Comment:* | | | | |

| | ALWAYS | OFTEN | SELDOM | RARELY |
|---|---|---|---|---|
| **Is Bullied** | ❍ | ❍ | ❍ | ❍ |
| *Comment:* | | | | |
| **Includes Others** | ❍ | ❍ | ❍ | ❍ |
| *Comment:* | | | | |
| **Honest** | ❍ | ❍ | ❍ | ❍ |
| *Comment:* | | | | |
| **Helpful** | ❍ | ❍ | ❍ | ❍ |
| *Comment:* | | | | |
| **Afraid** | ❍ | ❍ | ❍ | ❍ |
| *Comment:* | | | | |
| **Follows Rules** | ❍ | ❍ | ❍ | ❍ |
| *Comment:* | | | | |
| **Laughs** | ❍ | ❍ | ❍ | ❍ |
| *Comment:* | | | | |
| **Kind** | ❍ | ❍ | ❍ | ❍ |
| *Comment:* | | | | |
| **Likes Reading** | ❍ | ❍ | ❍ | ❍ |
| *Comment:* | | | | |
| **Talks Easily** | ❍ | ❍ | ❍ | ❍ |
| *Comment:* | | | | |
| **Bullies Others** | ❍ | ❍ | ❍ | ❍ |
| *Comment:* | | | | |
| **Gets Things Done** | ❍ | ❍ | ❍ | ❍ |
| *Comment:* | | | | |
| **Cooperates** | ❍ | ❍ | ❍ | ❍ |
| *Comment:* | | | | |
| **Lonely** | ❍ | ❍ | ❍ | ❍ |
| *Comment:* | | | | |

| | ALWAYS | OFTEN | SELDOM | RARELY |
|---|---|---|---|---|
| **Respected** | ❍ | ❍ | ❍ | ❍ |
| *Comment:* | | | | |
| **Happy** | ❍ | ❍ | ❍ | ❍ |
| *Comment:* | | | | |
| **Confident** | ❍ | ❍ | ❍ | ❍ |
| *Comment:* | | | | |
| **Patient** | ❍ | ❍ | ❍ | ❍ |
| *Comment:* | | | | |
| **Rude** | ❍ | ❍ | ❍ | ❍ |
| *Comment:* | | | | |
| **Works Well** | ❍ | ❍ | ❍ | ❍ |
| *Comment:* | | | | |
| **Tries** | ❍ | ❍ | ❍ | ❍ |
| *Comment:* | | | | |
| **Has Friends** | ❍ | ❍ | ❍ | ❍ |
| *Comment:* | | | | |
| **Orderly** | ❍ | ❍ | ❍ | ❍ |
| *Comment:* | | | | |
| **Isolated** | ❍ | ❍ | ❍ | ❍ |
| *Comment:* | | | | |
| **Safe** | ❍ | ❍ | ❍ | ❍ |
| *Comment:* | | | | |
| **Participates** | ❍ | ❍ | ❍ | ❍ |
| *Comment:* | | | | |
| **Team Work** | ❍ | ❍ | ❍ | ❍ |
| *Comment:* | | | | |
| **Moral** | ❍ | ❍ | ❍ | ❍ |
| *Comment:* | | | | |

| | ALWAYS | OFTEN | SELDOM | RARELY |
|---|---|---|---|---|
| **Respectful** | ❍ | ❍ | ❍ | ❍ |
| *Comment:* | | | | |
| **Has Goals** | ❍ | ❍ | ❍ | ❍ |
| *Comment:* | | | | |
| **Likes Math** | ❍ | ❍ | ❍ | ❍ |
| *Comment:* | | | | |
| **Hope For The Future** | ❍ | ❍ | ❍ | ❍ |
| *Comment:* | | | | |
| **Responsible** | ❍ | ❍ | ❍ | ❍ |
| *Comment:* | | | | |
| **Independent** | ❍ | ❍ | ❍ | ❍ |
| *Comment:* | | | | |
| **Adapts** | ❍ | ❍ | ❍ | ❍ |
| *Comment:* | | | | |
| **Good Citizen** | ❍ | ❍ | ❍ | ❍ |
| *Comment:* | | | | |
| **Successful** | ❍ | ❍ | ❍ | ❍ |
| *Comment:* | | | | |
| **Needed** | ❍ | ❍ | ❍ | ❍ |
| *Comment:* | | | | |
| **Worthwhile** | ❍ | ❍ | ❍ | ❍ |
| *Comment:* | | | | |
| **Cares** | ❍ | ❍ | ❍ | ❍ |
| *Comment:* | | | | |
| **Curious** | ❍ | ❍ | ❍ | ❍ |
| *Comment:* | | | | |
| **Tries Again** | ❍ | ❍ | ❍ | ❍ |
| *Comment:* | | | | |

# OVERVIEW COMMENTS:

# CHAPTER 43

## The Values Growth Chart – A Better Way of "Grading"

Life is a process of giving and receiving. I have devised the Values Growth Chart as a possible better model for a value-based grading system to build character and to build community values. Teachers, leaders, employers should feel free to improve or adapt it for their specific communities. It is as simple as asking the student, parent, and teacher to rate the student's progress in each category. The teacher's and parents' ratings should be written; the student's rating could be oral or written, but it should be recorded to serve in future evaluations. The benefit of using this chart to track growth is the thoughtful, real life discussion of important community values that will occur in school and at home between the teacher, parent, and student.

The Values Growth Chart is modeled after a basic physics principle: "every action has an equal and opposite reaction." The idea is that every person needs to both give and receive to attain a balance in life. It can be used with students from grade 3 through high school to track how they are progressing in development of life skills.

Consider the example of a gift. The giver of the gift feels a joy in their act of kindness. What the receiver of the gift does with the gift is their business. In general, we give gifts to be helpful to others. Letting go of the gift is part of the positive emotions we feel and retain. By the same token, receiving a gift has a certain expectation as well. Typically the receiver responds in a welcoming, gracious manner that respects the intent of the giver.

I envision the Values Growth Chart as a tool to encourage the "gift" of focused conversation. Any conversation is a balance of giving and receiving on a personal and emotional level. In the student and teacher setting, verbalizing the emotions and feelings that relate to ourselves and those around us helps us to make sense of our experiences. It helps us to find balance in our relationships and our lives.

The Values Growth Chart evaluation scale, on pages 117-121, is a model that is meant to reflect the values or characteristics that are valued in a certain community, company, or setting. As such, it will need to be adapted. I visualize that each setting would develop its own set of character traits to include in the template above. In the school setting, I see each school developing their own set of values with strong student involvement in the process so that the students "own" the values that are decided upon in the process. These values will need to be reviewed on a regular basis and should be open to modifications as needs change. Students and staff should be proud of their values, much like they are of their school spirit or school mascot.

***Life is a process of giving and receiving. I have devised the Values Growth Chart as a possible better model for a value-based grading system. Teachers, leaders, employers should feel free to improve or adapt it for their specific communities.***

Whether it is on the elementary, middle, or high school level, the teacher/mentor model of communication between home and school can really pay dividends. Annual teacher visits each summer can establish a cooperative, non-confrontational relationship between the home (parents and student) and the school. A few minutes dedicated to home visits can be the foundation of relationship building.

The benefit of utilizing the Values Growth Chart in parent-teacher conferences or by mailed to parents at home is in encouraging parent participation and communication in the education process. It may not always succeed because of complications, but it is an important first step to establish the meaningful, cooperative interaction that is critical in child development. It is a system that offers an opportunity to discover the loners, the isolated, or the unpopular to find inclusion in the education process.

*The Values Growth Chart evaluation scale is a model that is meant to reflect the values or characteristics that are valued in a certain community, company, or setting.*

Using the chart also affords teachers and families an early alert system for youngsters who are not fitting in or crying out for help or attention. These students can find great benefit in the work of community nonprofit personnel and mental health professionals as their young lives unfold. Having opportunities to socialize in normal and formative ways will benefit them in these foundational years, and hopefully save them from the being ostracized and lashing out at those around them.

The hope would be to help these young people grow up in normal, inclusive life settings and minimize the loneliness, depression, frustration, and abuse that seems to be becoming more visible these days.

This proposal suggests that education takes place for five hours a day and work takes place for five hours a day. The success of the Values Growth Chart will be evident at work and in relationships. The values need to be taught as part of the school curriculum and supported at work. For effective education each school should determine the courses in the five hour school session.

The problem is that without student engagement, education is not received and valued. Too many students are bored and distracted from disparities and a lack of interest in their future lives. Successful work will bring purpose and direction to life goals. Students will be changing the use of time from little supervision to a positive work environment. The Values Growth Chart should monitor behavioral attitudes for a period of eight to twelve years of education. We need to set up a system that demonstrates a student's desire to work. More on this later.

# CHAPTER 44

## The Values Growth Chart– A Springboard to Better Personal Growth

The Values Growth Chart described in the earlier chapter can be a superior way to draw the community together for a better educational outcome.

If you think about education from a consumer's viewpoint, who really is the consumer?

Is it the community?
Is it the parents?
Or is it the students?

You can make arguments for each of those constituencies, but maybe the single, clear focus needs to be the kids.

Let's face it. Lots of kids in the "Bottom Half" are not receiving an "equal serving" from their childhood experience. The factors are many. What is the parents' responsibility? What is the community's responsibility? Who is the community if it is not you and I? Technically, the community is not the public education system. Rather, it is a broad spectrum of the people that comprise that community, whether they be rich folks, poor folks, workers and bosses, politicians and voters, and so many more. Each community has their own sets of standards and goals.

Yet, under current practice, are we truly serving "Bottom Half" parents when we are assigning to educators the responsibility of providing their children with essentially all the training to help these children enter the work force and transition into a lifetime of work and citizenship where we expect them to be compassionate, caring neighbors in our community culture?

We need a better way. To me, this is where the Values Growth Chart can be so powerful. It is a tool that can easily be shared with parents. It offers a simple and visual way that parents can be involved in the educational process on a regular basis.

Once the student and the teacher/mentor fill out the chart, those charts can be shared with the parents so that parents can see both how their child views the values and how the teacher views the child's growth in these areas. Parents join the conversation and offer their insights into areas of growth or areas that need encouragement. I believe this could be a realistic way for academics to be combined with social and emotional growth to balance child development.

Parents should be encouraged to fill out the Values Growth Chart as well. This is what really brings family, school and the child together into the emotional growth picture. If the process can begin when the child enters the school system, all three key partners can track the child's growth into graduation. It is an early opportunity to observe and coach Social development. The child can be aware that behaviors matter while the school and the parents can be coached to work together on observing the child's self-image coupled with both parents and the school's observations on how the child fits into life around their social environment.

This may be a method that higher education should study over a period of years to find the best ways and practices of encouraging student growth in social skills and self-image.

To get back to my beginning point in this chapter, by focusing on the consumer, we can improve our educational systems. How can we be satisfied as a nation with a system that has a mere one-third of our students are doing math and reading at their proper grade level? There has to be a better way to do this. All of us learn in different ways. Teaching of basics, like math and reading, needs to be more flexible so that students can be successful and effective in these key areas of learning. We need our School Boards to step up and not simply represent the School Board's vision of school room success, but also to stand up for students of all levels, especially "Bottom Half" students who are struggling with learning disabilities and disparities.

Clearly looking at our existing educational system reveals that it is broken. The educational product being delivered to our children and teens (again especially our "Bottom Half" ones) is not working. Families, future employers, communities, and our nation are suffering as a result.

Work (honest, fair work) answers so many needs for teens trapped in this broken system. With so many of them unguided for hours and days at a time, so many doubting, lost, and drifting through lives alone and involved in negative habits and activities, we can help forge a new direction.

Compassion alone is not enough. We need inclusion by citizens like you and me. We need to begin the community conversation that will lead to making a difference in their lives and in ours. Incorporating a tool like the Values Growth Chart can open up that important conversation. It can guide a discussion of their thoughts and views and focus teens on society's status quo expectations. Even more, it can help them better face themselves and learn to see how others see them.

# CHAPTER 45

## Teach Teens How Money Works

How can families caught in the cycle of poverty escape their plight. Teaching them how to get their money to work for them is one answer.

Every young person I have ever talked to (and that is over a thousand students) has never even heard of the "rule of 72." That makes me think that their parents have never heard of, or understand, this important concept either.

Schools seem to be afraid of teaching the concept of money. Without understanding the basics of money, this makes it easy for banks, other financial institutions, and even insurance companies to take advantage of "Bottom Half" families.

It seems there are more than enough sources willing to loan them money via credit cards and car loans. The trap that many of the poor families find themselves in are that these sources force them into a PAY ME FIRST situation and often charge highly inflated interest rates that don't easily allow them to get out from under these "loans."

Money is not a scary topic, but we treat it that way. Of course, the people and institutions that have the money to loan want to maximize the highest return. This can lead to major problems for those who do not understand and thus are vulnerable and gullible.

Teaching low-income families and students how money gives you a certain kind of power is an important lesson that will pay dividends for them throughout their lives. When a family has money (or better yet, savings,) they have power. Power to make decisions, choices, and purchases. Power to be in control of their lives. With no money, the feeling of powerlessness to the circumstances around them is a harsh reality.

One of the first lessons that needs to be imparted is that it is not the size of a person's or family's income that matters, it is the size of their savings. In America, the concept goes back to Ben Franklin's famous proverbs.

A rich man has a penny left over at the end of the month; a poor man is a penny short. Or, a penny saved is a penny earned.

In America, this concept originated with Ben Franklin. And it still applies today! So often families spend their money on things that are "wants" or "the neat, new things" they see. All would be much better off if the spending went to real needs.

Debt never makes the future easier. Debt only measures lack of control and/or the measurement of circumstances.

# CHAPTER 46

## The Danger of "Wants"

Visit a rummage or garage sale. There are plenty of them around. It seems at almost any time of the year these days. What you will see is the "wants" of people. These trinkets are items that, at one point, they "had to have," but now are going for a quarter or 50 cents.

Did you realize that Americans have so much "stuff" that we have more storage facilities in the United States than fast food restaurants?

To be honest, we buy our kids their "wants." In so doing, we teach our children to "want" more. We do not promote frugality. We do not teach investing. Our young ones need to know why it pays off to invest when they are young. Today who knows or teaches why the values of thrift are important?

We can help everyone, especially those in the "Bottom Half," to be more successful by applying a few simple concepts. We need to . . .

1. teach thrift, frugality, and self-discipline in our finances.
2. demonstrate what being financially disciplined looks like and what it gets for those who practice it.
3. explain key terms like investing, savings accounts, annuities, stocks, bonds, mutual funds, index funds, ETFs, and the different types of life insurance options.
4. instruct about the concept of interest – the Rule of 72 – and how money can work for a person.
5. how to buy a car or a home

We claim to teach students math by sticking them in Algebra class. As a citizen and employer, I have heard the protests. Why do we need to learn this stuff that we will never use? I've also heard the teachers' answers and they are not too convincing to me.

Financial literacy is the math class that will make a difference in people's lives. It is practical, real-life problem solving. Instead of inane and impractical "word problems," imagine the long term value of having high school students figure out costs of buying a house, or whether it would be wiser to choose a condo than a house. What about renting or leasing an apartment. Would that be a better choice financially? How could buying a "fixer-upper" make a difference in their finances. Add to that the budgeting aspects of heat, light, water, real estate taxes. What is the total cost of home ownership? All practical problems that students will one day need to face.

Another practical financial question is the cost of transportation. What kind of car does a person need? What is the difference in cost if instead of the car I need, I buy the car I want? When is a car a good investment? Is leasing a good option? Compare costs of new vs. used cars? Is public transportation an option? How do car payments fit in a person's budget? What am I paying if I opt for long-term financing? How will gas prices or car repair bills affect my financial status? How much money could I save by alternate transportation like walking, biking and carpooling. Again all practical problems that all of us face daily.

They also need to dig into the concepts of investing and savings. What can a bank offer them? Is that better than a credit union or not? How does that compare to the stock market? Is investing in bonds a good choice? Imagine the learning that goes into the Stock Market Game that many schools offer. These offer great life lessons in success and failure.

Now this training shouldn't be a dull teacher lecture. Perhaps the kids could work in teams. Let them figure out the questions and the answers. Let them learn the real math of life.

# CHAPTER 47

## The Rule of 72

The Rule of 72 shows that money doubles as a function of 72.

6 years x 12% interest = 72

8 years x 9% interest = 72

9 years x 8% interest = 72

12 years x 6% interest = 72

Why is this important? Simply put, the higher the interest paid, the faster your money doubles.

Take one example. Assume a 15-year-old invests $1000. The chart below illustrates what is possible if that investment is left to accumulate. Notice how the different interest rates affect the investment and bottom line.

| 6% Interest | | 8% Interest | | 10% Interest | | 12% Interest | |
|---|---|---|---|---|---|---|---|
| 15 | $1000 | 15 | $1000 | 15 | $1000 | 15 | $1000 |
| 27 | $2000 | 24 | $2000 | 22 | $2000 | 21 | $2000 |
| 39 | $4000 | 33 | $4000 | 29.2 | $4000 | 27 | $4000 |
| 51 | $8000 | 42 | $8000 | 36.4 | $8000 | 33 | $8000 |
| 63 | $16,000 | 51 | $16,000 | 43.6 | $16,000 | 39 | $16,000 |
| *Investment doubles every 12 years - 5 doubles | | 60 | $32,000 | 50.8 | $32,000 | 45 | $32,000 |
| | | *Investment doubles every 9 years - 6 doubles | | 58 | $64,000 | 51 | $64,000 |
| | | | | 65.2 | $128,000 | 57 | $128,000 |
| | | | | *Investment doubles every 7.2 years - 8 doubles | | 63 | $256,000 |
| | | | | | | *Investment doubles every 6 years - 9 doubles | |

If more people understood "The Rule of 72," it would revolutionize how families would choose to invest their money. Stockbrokers, banks, and insurance professionals would not be able to make the rich salaries they pay to their top people as they skim percentages off investments during the management of the funds of their customers.

Warren Buffet advises everyday citizens how to beat this system. He advises that people invest in No Fee - Low Cost - Index Funds. (Low cost is defined as less than 1% cost per year.) These funds mirror the performance of the Dow Jones Industrial Average, the S & P 500, or similar large index funds.

Buffet suggests that over the past forty years, that if dividends and interest are reinvested and the principal would be left untouched, these investments would double every 5.91 years at a 12.29% return. What this means is that if a parent would set aside $1000 in such an investment at the birth of their child, by age 66 that investment would have grown to over $2 million dollars. Who wouldn't want to provide that kind of security for their children?

# CHAPTER 48

## Failure as a Learning Experience

There's a wonderful book by Jessica Lakey entitled The Gift of Failure. An important concept that she features is that some of the best learning comes as a result of failure.

The point is that students are more successful in learning life if they explore and come up with their own conclusions. This is really true of all of us. Nobody likes to be told what to think and why to think it. A value of this proposed apprenticeship program is that it puts students in charge of their experience in a real way.

As part of the apprenticeship employment process, the students will be choosing and applying for the jobs they want. The choices should not be made by teachers or parents. Each student needs to be invested in the process. The steps needs to be genuine, personal and authentic. In that way, the student develops their self-image, learns resilience, and praise for their efforts.

*Nobody likes to told what to think and why to think it. A value of this proposed apprenticeship program is that it puts students in charge of their experience in a real way.*

"That was challenging! You worked diligently and did a great job." These are responses that will build character in "Bottom Half" students and motivate them to continue to do well. Students are starved for responsibility, support, and success. Poor grades become detrimental for "Bottom Half" students. Taking risks, building a strong work ethic, gaining self-confidence, and decision-making skills will be the results for students in the apprentice program. The students will take these qualities with them throughout their lives.

There should be no grades for work. Apprentices will do better, with higher levels of interest, if they make their own way to their own ends. In Lakey's words, "Let them have flaws." All of us have flaws. That is what makes us unique in our character as individuals. Our struggles and even failures are what encourage resilience on future tasks and challenges.

We cannot be afraid to allow teens fail. At times they will stumble just as we do. Maturity can be defined as how well people handle their challenges. Let teens learn and build on these important lessons.

## TAKEAWAYS FOR DISCUSSION:

# CHAPTER 49

## Just Do It!
## The Short, Sweet Action Plan

The joy of giving the "Bottom Half" an opportunity to find success, personal purpose, and stability in life is clear.

It does not cost families, schools, businesses, or the community any extra money.

We do not need complicated rationales, formulas, or philosophies. We do not need prolonged debates. School leaders and school boards can move this proposal ahead quickly because it builds on recognized efforts that are already successful. This plan expands existing programs to make a difference in more lives than ever before.

Parents and kids, especially "Bottom Half" families: tell your schools we want to work and what kind of work you we want in our future. Employers and community leaders: we can listen and make this happen.

All we have to do is form a task force and get started. Let's "get down to business" and find jobs, jobs that provide future opportunities for "Bottom Half" teens.

This is a legal and practical solution to a real problem in our culture and society. Education leaders like Wisconsin Department of Public Instruction and now Governor Tony Evers and former Governor Scott Walker encourage apprenticeship programs.

It would be a step in the right direction for “Bottom half” teens in any high school among the eleven in the Fox Cities ... or for that matter, any high school in the country.

Be a hero. Form a task force. Advocate for Bottom Half teens. Make a difference in their future and our future.

**Just do it!**

# CHAPTER 50

## The Fox Cities & Beyond ...

This short book was written with the Fox Cities in mind. At the same time, the principles of this book can be applied to cities across America. Implementing the Fox Cities Action Plan for Apprenticeships will be transformative for our communities.

I believe this model or pattern is easily transportable. It is in light of this dream that resource pages are being added to the book. The numbers speak for themselves. As stated earlier, the cost of failure is very expensive ... financially, emotionally, and socially.

These charts and statistics clearly illustrate a very high price tag. If this proposal has moved you to action, take a close look at these pages. The information here is readily available to those who care. We are sharing the numbers that apply to the Fox Cities community, but every community has unique characteristics which can be studied and used to make a difference in the lives of the children of those communities.

As word gets out about this inspired approach, it is my hope that interested leaders will take these resource pages and find out just what is happening in their own communities. Those figures might be better or worse, higher or lower, than what is found here. The key is to find those numbers and confront the reality of the struggle of the "Bottom Half Teens" in your community.

**America's Rank:**

**Income and Wealth**
1st for number of billionaires, 2017

**Key Child Outcomes**
30th for percent of children in poverty, 2015

- Children's Defense Fund

# CHAPTER 51

## Some Cautions and a Look at History ... and Hope

First, the apprenticeship program will not work for every student, but for the 200 from each of the three high school classes, the opportunities for success will, in most cases, lead to significant positive changes both in the students' high school years and their future as adults. We can do so much better for our teens, especially our "Bottom Half Teens!"

The teen years are undoubtedly among the most challenging in a person's life. Curiosity about what the future holds fills us with dreams and expectations. These are years of tremendous growth. Fill these years with positive attitudes and achievements, build self-confidence and pride in one's self which will lead to dreams fulfilled in many lives. Find ways to maximize this opportunity for our youth between ages 13 and 23 will set these young adults and our culture on the path to future success.

Look back 100 years. It was a time of youth being raised on farms with chores to do. Fifty years ago some still worked on farms, but many were growing up in the city. Paper routes, shoveling snow for neighbors, and babysitting were the common chores of that period. It makes sense today to replace these chores with apprenticeships.

Europe offers a pattern worth reviewing. At the end of World War II, the countries of Europe were in shambles. Their economies were broken, factories destroyed, and families shattered. Work and food were desperate needs. What was to be done? There were not enough young men to rebuild the shattered economies of these war-torn countries.

With significant help from the Marshall Plan, the people in Europe had the opportunity to go back to work, put food on their tables, and receive medical services. These countries moved from mere survival to times of success.

In the process, Europeans developed a school system in which students who did not meet certain academic standards were moved into working in apprenticeship programs. No shame. No negatives. Students were prized for their skills as important future workers and trained in those roles through teen apprenticeships.

Today with Baby Boomers retiring at a rapid rate, our country needs young workers to keep our work force vibrant. Just as they did in the post-WWII climate in Europe, our teens can provide the talent, strength, and enthusiasm.

Think about it. Mom and dads, who do you turn to for help when your computer is giving you problems? Of course ... your kids! Where do modern employers need the most help? They need help with computers and highly automated control operating machinery. Do you think teens can handle it? Look at those who are performing many of the service roles in businesses today which include fast food restaurants, coffee shops, convenience stores, malls and department stores. In many cases, jobs are done by high school students.

Truly they are capable. Imagine how these young people can be prepared even more effectively to take their place in our society and find success when communities grasp the opportunity offered by apprenticeship programs!

# CHAPTER 52

## Nothing happens until somebody moves

This book asks each community in America to take a serious look at their Bottom Half teens to see if their futures truly allow for a productive work life and good citizenship. Is what we're doing now putting them in a position to build families and lead productive lives?

Somebody, or better yet, somebodies, in each community will need to make a move.

In 1965, retired business executive Bill Kellett of Neenah, Wisconsin brought together 532 state wide business leaders to work toward more efficient government, saving the state $34 million per year. In 1966, he chaired the Reorganization of State Government Committee, in the process reducing the number of state agencies from 96 to 28. He also chaired Governor Knowles' Commission on Education. We need that kind of leadership again.

Who will be the leaders willing to step up now to bring about educational reforms in each of our communities?

It is many of the "Bottom Half Teens" of today who will be unemployed, reeling from unstable childhood experiences or otherwise in need of public assistance tomorrow. If we do nothing now, more and more public dollars will be needed to deal with them on the back end, be it welfare or health care subsidies or incarceration.

Change on the front end has to happen. We have to provide an avenue where the possibility of success is there. We can't wait for the government to do it for us. The politicians of today have shown that they are incapable of major, positive American culture changes. It takes ordinary citizens willing to stand up and be heard to lead significant cultural change in their communities.

We can do that by providing a realistic path for our "Bottom Half Teens." We need to give them the opportunity, show them a path that makes sense and a goal that is within reach. We must show them the benefits of engaging in their own lives. In the process we teach them the benefits of hard work and the values of working and living in this world together.

So, how do we do that?

First, we need to build awareness that these teens can be motivated and engaged in life. We need to spur widespread discussion groups in our communities. It starts with one and builds from there. Gather a group of four or five or six people who care about kids and have a desire for change. Read this book and discuss the various chapters. Challenge each member of your group to begin an additional discussion group on a selected topic.

Keep that going as the chain of discussion groups grows. Soon you have dozens, then hundreds, maybe thousands of people in your community talking about change. A movement is born.

Then identify 20 or so passionate leaders who can keep the conversation moving forward. That becomes your oversight committee. Pull together recommendations that have come from those discussion groups. Then engage with civic leaders and local media as you present detailed recommendations from the committee and push for implementation.

The process must be inclusive, and you'll need to gain a measure of consensus. Perhaps an advisory referendum would be in play to gain even wider feedback from the community.

Be sure to engage students and parents in the process, as well as business leaders, service organizations, nonprofits. People from all segments of the local population need to be part of the conversation.

That's not easy, of course. One of the challenges in forming diverse discussion groups is getting buy in from that Bottom Half community. These are people who might be dealing with evictions or other housing issues, perhaps parenting alone and under stressful conditions, or struggling with mental health issues, under employment or facing other challenging circumstances. They may not hear what you're saying or believe that their opinion matters.

*There is not a blueprint for these public discussions. Each group and each community is unique. Your groups need to be inclusive. What comes from those conversations will frame the path you take.*

Seek out their ideas. If you can get them into a small group discussion, make a point before the meeting ends to ask each member for comments. Make sure they know their input in valuable. If they are withdrawn at first, chances are good they will become more comfortable and willing to share as the process evolves.

There is not a blueprint for these public discussions. Each group and each community is unique. Your groups need to be inclusive. What comes from those conversations will frame the path you take.

We can learn lessons from our founding fathers. In her book, "American Scripture: Making the Declaration of Independence," author Pauline Maier details how the gathering of consensus provided the backbone of what would become a united vision for independence. It is not hard to imagine the range and depth of opinions as the calls went out across the 13 colonies asking to pledge their lives and fortunes, in writing for building an army if necessary and their acceptance of the financial consequences of separating the

13 colonial economonies from England. More than 90 versions of declarations of independence are on record.

The versions and the sophistications varied, but they all clearly sought the same thing. And it all came through consensus building. No wonder they were able to raise an Army that went through such terrible hardship in the succeeding years and maintained great commitment throughout.

Consensus building is as relevant today as it was in the days of Thomas Jefferson. We need to have the will to not only begin the process but to see it through.

Now, let's get to work and move the entire community forward. We cannot be satisfied with the current cycle of poverty that leaves so many of our children without a path to a productive adult life.

In each community, it takes one person to be the spark to start a movement, to begin a consensus that will hopefully rescue young lives trapped in a broken system.

# TAKEAWAYS FOR ACTION:

Appendex — Selected Reports

# ALICE:
# A Study of Financial Hardship in Wisconsin

2018 reports

ALICE® is an acronym for Asset Limited, Income Constrained, Employed.

The United Way *ALICE Project* is a collaboration of United Ways in Connecticut, Florida, Hawai'i, Idaho, Indiana, Iowa, Louisiana, Maryland, Michigan, New Jersey, New York, Ohio, Oregon, Texas, Virginia, Washington, and Wisconsin.

# THE UNITED WAY ALICE PROJECT

The United Way *ALICE Project* provides a framework, language, and tools to measure and understand the struggles of a population called **ALICE** — an acronym for **A**sset **L**imited, **I**ncome **C**onstrained, **E**mployed. ALICE is the growing number of households in our communities that do not earn enough to afford basic necessities. This research initiative partners with state United Way organizations to present data that can stimulate meaningful discussion, attract new partners, and ultimately inform strategies for positive change.

Based on the overwhelming success of this research in identifying and articulating the needs of this vulnerable population, the United Way *ALICE Project* has grown from a pilot in Morris County, New Jersey in 2009, to the entire state of New Jersey in 2012, and now to the national level with 18 states participating. United Way of Wisconsin is proud to join the more than 540 United Ways in these states that are working to better understand ALICE's struggles. Organizations across the country are also using this data to address the challenges and needs of their employees, customers, and communities. The result is that ALICE is rapidly becoming part of the common vernacular, appearing in the media and in public forums discussing financial hardship in communities nationwide.

Together, United Ways, government agencies, nonprofits, and corporations have the opportunity to evaluate current initiatives and discover innovative approaches that give ALICE a voice, and create changes that improve life for ALICE and the wider community.

To access reports from all states, visit UnitedWayALICE.org

## States With United Way ALICE Reports

# AT-A-GLANCE: WISCONSIN

**2016 Point-in-Time Data**

**Population:** 5,778,709 | **Number of Counties:** 72 | **Number of Households:** 2,326,846

## How many households are struggling?

**ALICE**, an acronym for **A**sset **L**imited, **I**ncome **C**onstrained, **E**mployed, are households that earn more than the Federal Poverty Level (FPL), but less than the basic cost of living for the state (the ALICE Threshold). Of Wisconsin's 2,326,846 households, 271,935 earn below the FPL (11.7 percent) and another 600,626 (25.8 percent) are ALICE households.

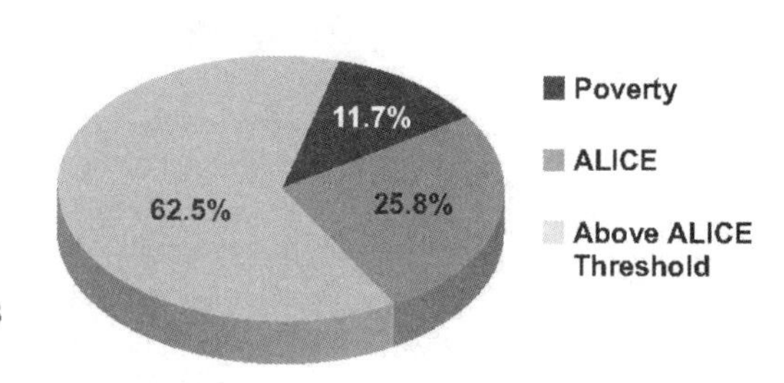


## How much does ALICE earn?

**In Wisconsin, 62 percent of jobs pay less than $20 per hour, with more than half of those paying less than $15 per hour.** Another 32 percent of jobs pay between $20 and $40 per hour. Less than 6 percent of jobs pay more than $40 per hour.

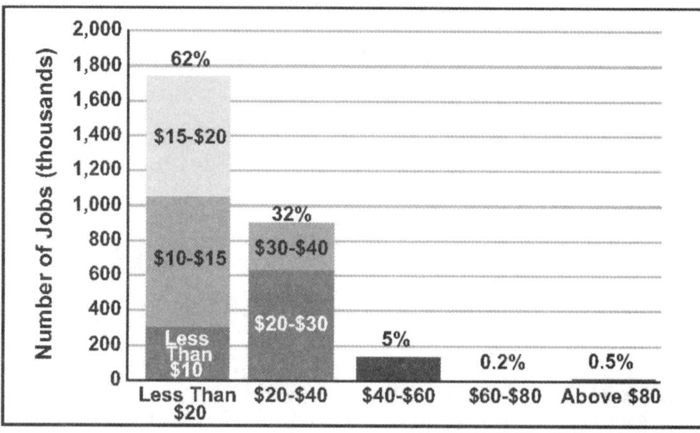


## What does it cost to afford the basic necessities?

Despite low national inflation during the recovery (9 percent from 2010 to 2016), the bare-minimum Household Survival Budget increased by 18 percent for a family and 24 percent for a single adult. Affording only a very modest living, this budget is still significantly more than the Federal Poverty Level of $11,880 for a single adult and $24,300 for a family of four.

| Household Survival Budget, Wisconsin Average, 2016 | | |
|---|---|---|
| | SINGLE ADULT | 2 ADULTS, 1 INFANT, 1 PRESCHOOLER |
| Monthly Costs | | |
| Housing | $492 | $735 |
| Child Care | $– | $1,231 |
| Food | $158 | $525 |
| Transportation | $349 | $698 |
| Health Care | $215 | $802 |
| Technology* | $55 | $75 |
| Miscellaneous | $150 | $467 |
| Taxes | $235 | $602 |
| Monthly Total | $1,654 | $5,135 |
| ANNUAL TOTAL | $19,848 | $61,620 |
| *Hourly Wage*** | *$9.92* | *$30.81* |

**New to budget in 2016*

***Full-time wage required to support this budget*

# I. ALICE BY THE NUMBERS

In 2016, six years after the end of the Great Recession, many households in Wisconsin were still struggling to find jobs with high enough wages and long enough hours to cover their basic monthly household expenses. More than one in three households in Wisconsin (37.5 percent) could not afford basic needs such as housing, child care, food, transportation, health care, and a smartphone. While many of Wisconsin's households were living below the Federal Poverty Level (FPL), an even greater number were households with incomes above the FPL, but not high enough to afford basic necessities. These households are **ALICE: A**sset **L**imited, **I**ncome **C**onstrained, **E**mployed.

This section drills down further to reveal the demographics of ALICE and poverty-level households by age, race/ethnicity, and household type over time. Also reported are important local variations that are often masked by state averages. The first United Way ALICE Report for Wisconsin, published in 2016 with 2014 data, showed that during the Recession there was an increase in the number of households with income below the ALICE Threshold, increasing from 35 percent in 2007 to 36 percent in 2010. This Report focuses on how Wisconsin residents fared post-Recession, from 2010 to 2016. While the overall economic climate has improved since 2010, the number of ALICE and poverty-level households rose to 37.5 percent of all Wisconsin households by 2016.

## OVERVIEW

In Wisconsin, the total number of households increased by 2 percent between 2010 and 2016 to 2,326,846. But the number of ALICE and poverty-level households increased by even more (5 percent) (Figure 1):

- **Poverty:** The number of households in poverty — defined as those earning at or below $11,880 for a single adult and $24,300 for a family of four — rose very slightly from 271,832 in 2010 to 271,935 in 2016. The proportion of poverty-level households fluctuated between 11.7 and 12.5 percent during the period.
- **ALICE:** The number of ALICE households rose from 559,808 in 2010 to 600,626 in 2016, a 7 percent increase. The proportion of ALICE households rose from 24.5 percent to 25.8 percent during that period.

### Figure 1.
### Household Income, Wisconsin, 2010 to 2016

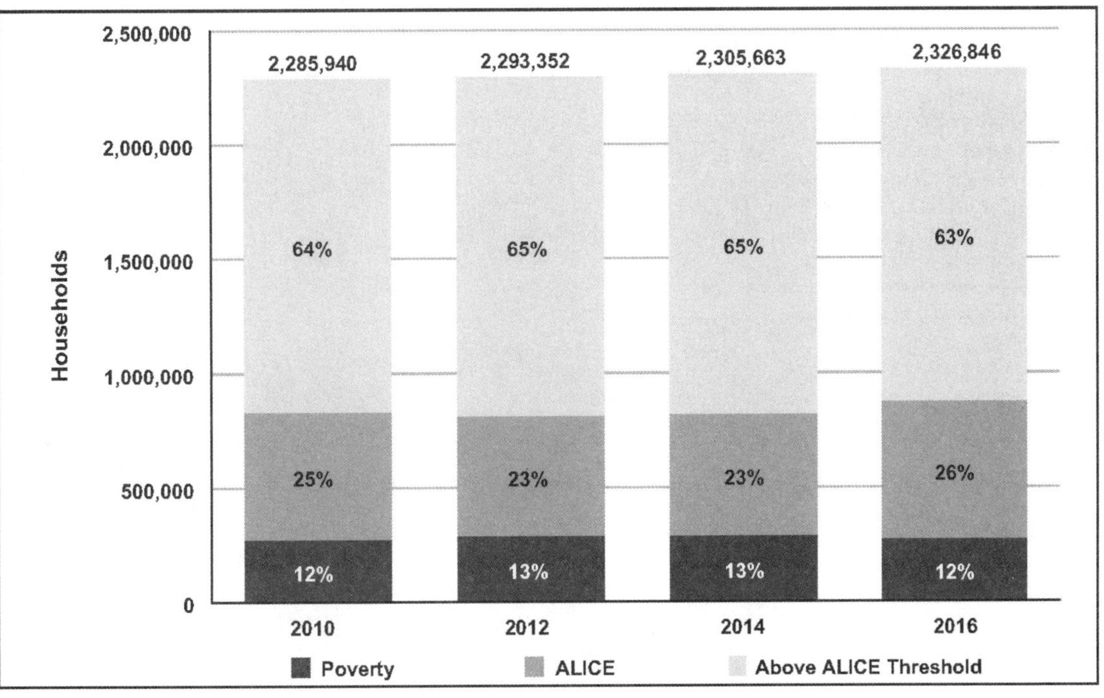


*Source: American Community Survey, 2007-2016, and the ALICE Threshold, 2007-2016. For the Methodology Overview and additional data, visit our website: UnitedWayALICE.org*

# ALICE IN BROWN COUNTY

**2016 Point-in-Time Data**

**Population:** 260,401 • **Number of Households:** 104,804
**Median Household Income:** $57,783 (state average: $56,811)
**Unemployment Rate:** 3% (state average: 4.1%)
**ALICE Households:** 24% (state average: 25.8%) • **Households in Poverty:** 10% (state average: 11.7%)

## How has the number of ALICE households changed over time?

**ALICE** is an acronym for **A**sset **L**imited, **I**ncome **C**onstrained, **E**mployed – households that earn more than the Federal Poverty Level, but less than the basic cost of living for the county (the ALICE Threshold). Combined, the number of ALICE and poverty-level households equals the total population struggling to afford basic needs. The number of households below the ALICE Threshold changes over time; households move in and out of poverty and ALICE status as their circumstances improve or worsen. The recovery, which started in 2010, has been uneven across the state. Conditions have improved for some families, but with rising costs, many still find themselves struggling.

### Households by Income, 2010 to 2016

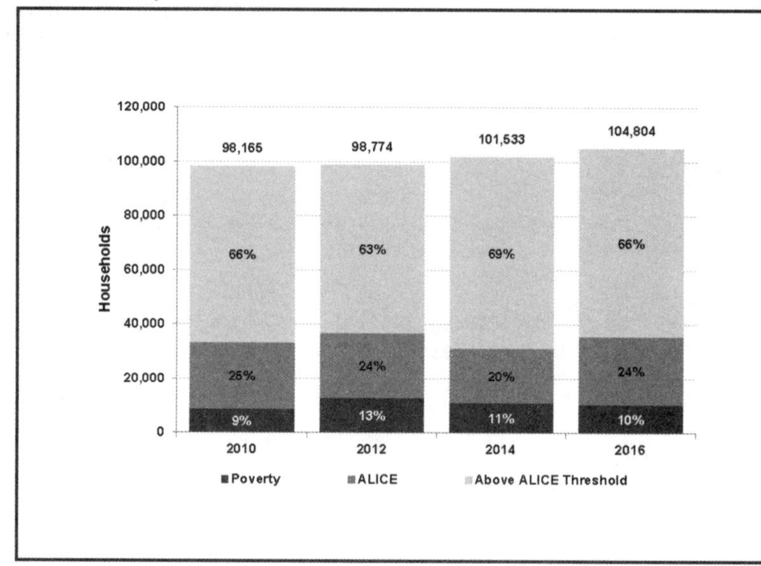


## What types of households are struggling?

The way Americans live is changing. There are more different family and living combinations than ever before, including more adults living alone, with roommates, or with their parents. Families with children are changing: There are more non-married cohabiting parents, same-sex parents, and blended families with remarried parents. The number of senior households is also increasing. Yet all types of households continue to struggle: ALICE and poverty-level households exist across all of these living arrangements.

### Household Types by Income, 2016

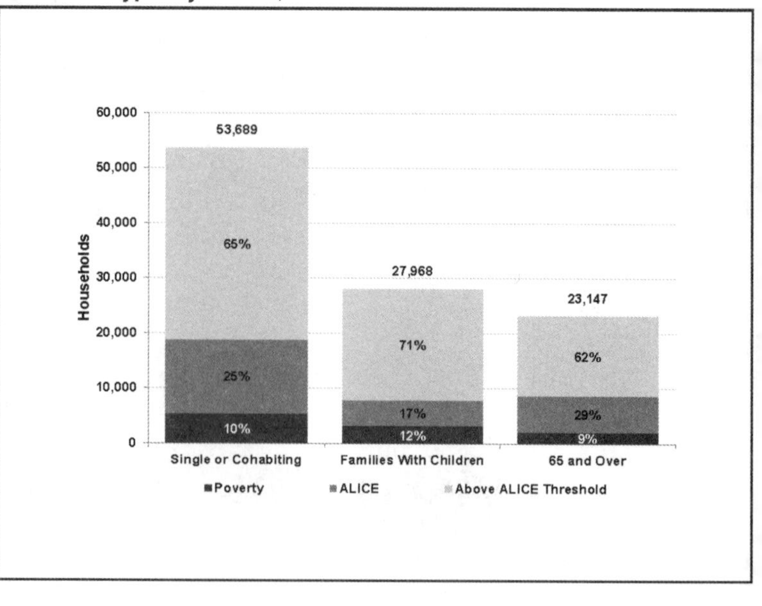

# Why do so many households struggle?

**The cost of living continues to increase...**

The Household Survival Budget reflects the bare minimum that a household needs to live and work today. It does not include savings for emergencies or future goals like college. In 2016, costs were well above the Federal Poverty Level of $11,880 for a single adult and $24,300 for a family of four. Family costs increased by 18 percent statewide from 2010 to 2016, compared to 9 percent inflation nationally.

| Household Survival Budget, Brown County | | |
|---|---|---|
| | SINGLE ADULT | 2 ADULTS, 1 INFANT, 1 PRESCHOOLER |
| Monthly Costs | | |
| Housing | $466 | $756 |
| Child Care | $– | $1,330 |
| Food | $158 | $525 |
| Transportation | $349 | $697 |
| Health Care | $214 | $800 |
| Technology | $55 | $75 |
| Miscellaneous | $147 | $483 |
| Taxes | $225 | $650 |
| Monthly Total | $1,614 | $5,316 |
| ANNUAL TOTAL | $19,368 | $63,792 |
| *Hourly Wage* | *$9.68* | *$31.90* |

**...and wages lag behind**

Employment and wages vary by location; firms generally pay higher wages in areas with a higher cost of living, although those wages still do not always cover basic needs. Employment and wages also vary by firm size: Large firms tend to offer higher wages and more job stability; smaller businesses can account for more jobs overall, especially in rural areas, but may pay less and offer less stability. Medium-size firms pay more but typically employ the fewest workers.

## Private-Sector Employment by Firm Size With Average Annual Wages, 2016

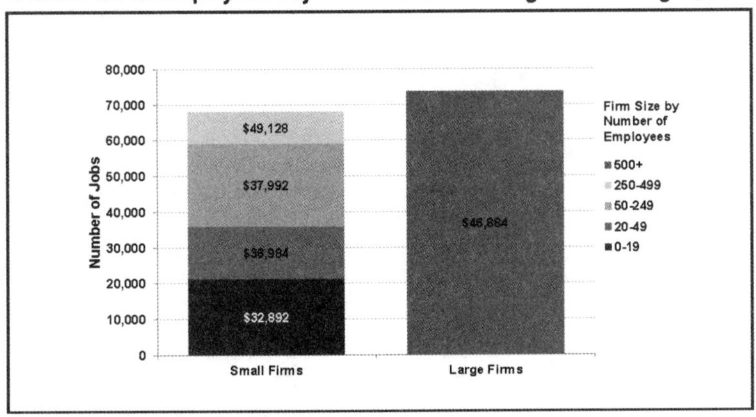


*Sources: **2016 Point-in-Time Data**: American Community Survey. **ALICE Demographics:** American Community Survey; the ALICE Threshold. **Budget:** U.S. Department of Housing and Urban Development; U.S. Department of Agriculture; Bureau of Labor Statistics; Internal Revenue Service; Tax Foundation; and Wisconsin Department of Children and Families, 2016.*

| Brown County, 2016 | | |
|---|---|---|
| Town | Total HH | % ALICE & Poverty |
| Allouez village | 5,308 | 26% |
| Ashwaubenon village | 7,593 | 38% |
| Bellevue village | 6,327 | 37% |
| De Pere city | 9,465 | 30% |
| Denmark village | 872 | 39% |
| Eaton | 551 | 16% |
| Glenmore | 415 | 21% |
| Green Bay | 782 | 15% |
| Green Bay city | 42,521 | 48% |
| Hobart village | 2,812 | 28% |
| Holland | 523 | 21% |
| Howard village | 7,536 | 31% |
| Humboldt | 487 | 21% |
| Lawrence | 1,874 | 18% |
| Ledgeview | 2,755 | 22% |
| Morrison | 564 | 23% |
| New Denmark | 564 | 22% |
| Pittsfield | 967 | 16% |
| Pulaski village | 1,445 | 40% |
| Rockland | 605 | 13% |
| Scott | 1,500 | 16% |
| Suamico village | 4,475 | 18% |
| Wrightstown | 852 | 25% |
| Wrightstown village | 1,095 | 26% |

*Note: Municipal-level data on this page is 5-year averages for Census Places and County Subdivisions. Totals will not always match county-level numbers because some county-level data is 1-year estimates.*

# ALICE IN CALUMET COUNTY

**2016 Point-in-Time Data**

**Population:** 49,653 • **Number of Households:** 18,839
**Median Household Income:** $70,042 (state average: $56,811)
**Unemployment Rate:** 3% (state average: 4.1%)
**ALICE Households:** 22% (state average: 25.8%) • **Households in Poverty:** 7% (state average: 11.7%)

## How has the number of ALICE households changed over time?

**ALICE** is an acronym for **A**sset **L**imited, **I**ncome **C**onstrained, **E**mployed – households that earn more than the Federal Poverty Level, but less than the basic cost of living for the county (the ALICE Threshold). Combined, the number of ALICE and poverty-level households equals the total population struggling to afford basic needs. The number of households below the ALICE Threshold changes over time; households move in and out of poverty and ALICE status as their circumstances improve or worsen. The recovery, which started in 2010, has been uneven across the state. Conditions have improved for some families, but with rising costs, many still find themselves struggling.

### Households by Income, 2010 to 2016

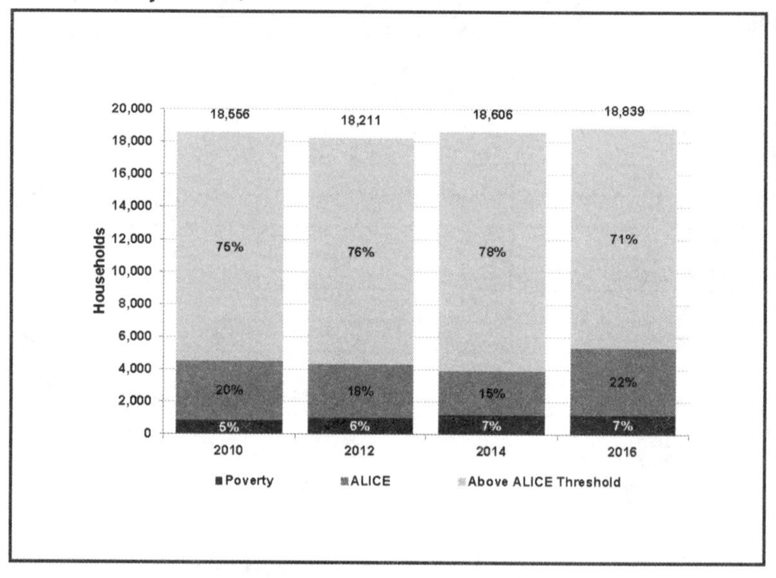


## What types of households are struggling?

The way Americans live is changing. There are more different family and living combinations than ever before, including more adults living alone, with roommates, or with their parents. Families with children are changing: There are more non-married cohabiting parents, same-sex parents, and blended families with remarried parents. The number of senior households is also increasing. Yet all types of households continue to struggle: ALICE and poverty-level households exist across all of these living arrangements.

### Household Types by Income, 2016

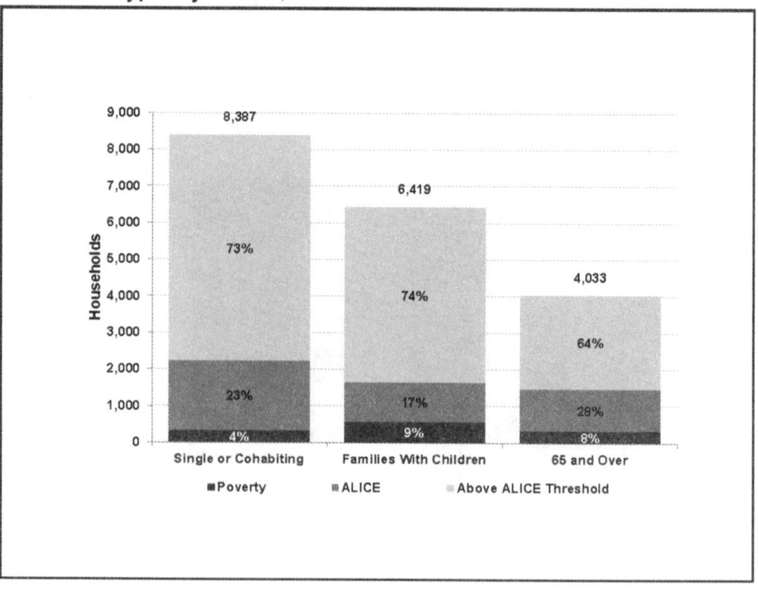

# Why do so many households struggle?

**The cost of living continues to increase...**

The Household Survival Budget reflects the bare minimum that a household needs to live and work today. It does not include savings for emergencies or future goals like college. In 2016, costs were well above the Federal Poverty Level of $11,880 for a single adult and $24,300 for a family of four. Family costs increased by 18 percent statewide from 2010 to 2016, compared to 9 percent inflation nationally.

| Household Survival Budget, Calumet County | | |
|---|---|---|
| | SINGLE ADULT | 2 ADULTS, 1 INFANT, 1 PRESCHOOLER |
| Monthly Costs | | |
| Housing | $443 | $718 |
| Child Care | $– | $1,315 |
| Food | $158 | $525 |
| Transportation | $349 | $697 |
| Health Care | $214 | $800 |
| Technology | $55 | $75 |
| Miscellaneous | $144 | $476 |
| Taxes | $218 | $628 |
| Monthly Total | $1,581 | $5,234 |
| ANNUAL TOTAL | $18,972 | $62,808 |
| *Hourly Wage* | *$9.49* | *$31.40* |

**...and wages lag behind**

Employment and wages vary by location; firms generally pay higher wages in areas with a higher cost of living, although those wages still do not always cover basic needs. Employment and wages also vary by firm size: Large firms tend to offer higher wages and more job stability; smaller businesses can account for more jobs overall, especially in rural areas, but may pay less and offer less stability. Medium-size firms pay more but typically employ the fewest workers.

## Private-Sector Employment by Firm Size With Average Annual Wages, 2016

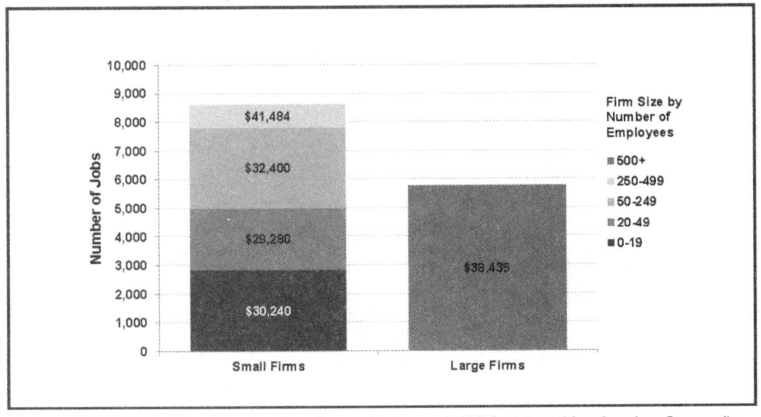


*Sources: **2016 Point-in-Time Data**: American Community Survey. **ALICE Demographics:** American Community Survey; the ALICE Threshold. **Budget:** U.S. Department of Housing and Urban Development; U.S. Department of Agriculture; Bureau of Labor Statistics; Internal Revenue Service; Tax Foundation; and Wisconsin Department of Children and Families, 2016.*

| Calumet County, 2016 | | |
|---|---|---|
| Town | Total HH | % ALICE & Poverty |
| Appleton city | 4,264 | 33% |
| Brillion | 624 | 36% |
| Brillion city | 1,157 | 32% |
| Brothertown | 538 | 32% |
| Charlestown | 293 | 27% |
| Chilton | 406 | 21% |
| Chilton city | 1,622 | 41% |
| Harrison | 469 | 12% |
| Harrison village | 3,315 | 12% |
| Hilbert village | 467 | 52% |
| Kiel city | 122 | 54% |
| Menasha city | 894 | 26% |
| New Holstein | 595 | 33% |
| New Holstein city | 1,426 | 41% |
| Potter village | 103 | 33% |
| Rantoul | 272 | 21% |
| Sherwood village | 1,016 | 15% |
| Stockbridge | 590 | 26% |
| Stockbridge village | 321 | 30% |
| Woodville | 345 | 23% |

*Note: Municipal-level data on this page is 5-year averages for Census Places and County Subdivisions. Totals will not always match county-level numbers because some county-level data is 1-year estimates.*

# ALICE IN OUTAGAMIE COUNTY

**2016 Point-in-Time Data**

**Population:** 184,526 • **Number of Households:** 72,994
**Median Household Income:** $61,149 (state average: $56,811)
**Unemployment Rate:** 4% (state average: 4.1%)
**ALICE Households:** 22% (state average: 25.8%) • **Households in Poverty:** 8% (state average: 11.7%)

## How has the number of ALICE households changed over time?

**ALICE** is an acronym for **A**sset **L**imited, **I**ncome **C**onstrained, **E**mployed – households that earn more than the Federal Poverty Level, but less than the basic cost of living for the county (the ALICE Threshold). Combined, the number of ALICE and poverty-level households equals the total population struggling to afford basic needs. The number of households below the ALICE Threshold changes over time; households move in and out of poverty and ALICE status as their circumstances improve or worsen. The recovery, which started in 2010, has been uneven across the state. Conditions have improved for some families, but with rising costs, many still find themselves struggling.

### Households by Income, 2010 to 2016

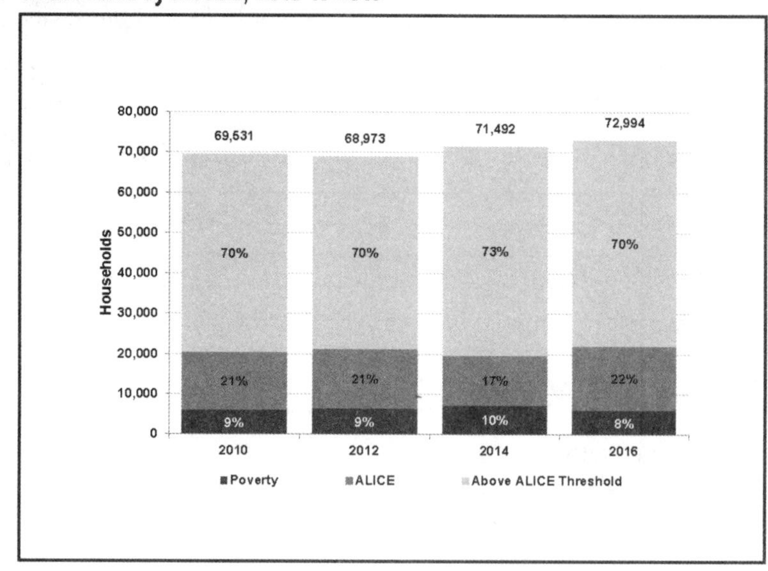


## What types of households are struggling?

The way Americans live is changing. There are more different family and living combinations than ever before, including more adults living alone, with roommates, or with their parents. Families with children are changing: There are more non-married cohabiting parents, same-sex parents, and blended families with remarried parents. The number of senior households is also increasing. Yet all types of households continue to struggle: ALICE and poverty-level households exist across all of these living arrangements.

### Household Types by Income, 2016

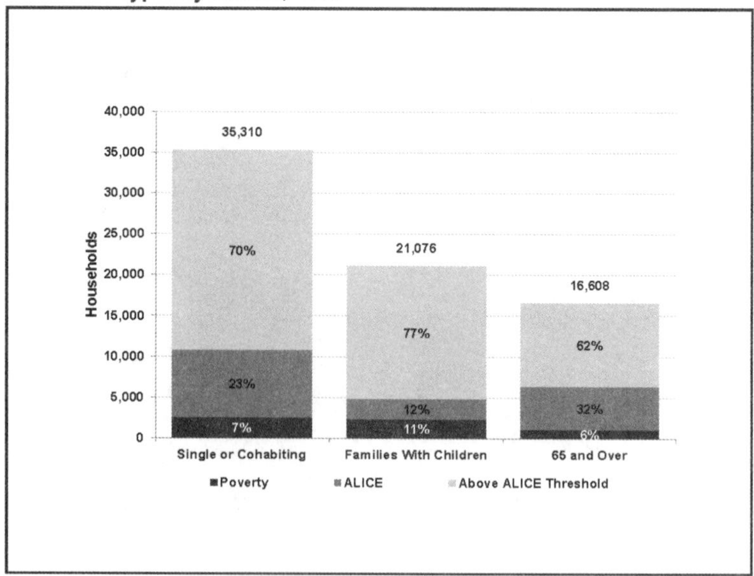

# Why do so many households struggle?

**The cost of living continues to increase...**

The Household Survival Budget reflects the bare minimum that a household needs to live and work today. It does not include savings for emergencies or future goals like college. In 2016, costs were well above the Federal Poverty Level of $11,880 for a single adult and $24,300 for a family of four. Family costs increased by 18 percent statewide from 2010 to 2016, compared to 9 percent inflation nationally.

| Household Survival Budget, Outagamie County | | |
|---|---|---|
| | SINGLE ADULT | 2 ADULTS, 1 INFANT, 1 PRESCHOOLER |
| Monthly Costs | | |
| Housing | $443 | $718 |
| Child Care | $– | $1,425 |
| Food | $158 | $525 |
| Transportation | $349 | $697 |
| Health Care | $214 | $800 |
| Technology | $55 | $75 |
| Miscellaneous | $144 | $491 |
| Taxes | $218 | $673 |
| Monthly Total | $1,581 | $5,404 |
| ANNUAL TOTAL | $18,972 | $64,848 |
| *Hourly Wage* | *$9.49* | *$32.42* |

**...and wages lag behind**

Employment and wages vary by location; firms generally pay higher wages in areas with a higher cost of living, although those wages still do not always cover basic needs. Employment and wages also vary by firm size: Large firms tend to offer higher wages and more job stability; smaller businesses can account for more jobs overall, especially in rural areas, but may pay less and offer less stability. Medium-size firms pay more but typically employ the fewest workers.

## Private-Sector Employment by Firm Size With Average Annual Wages, 2016

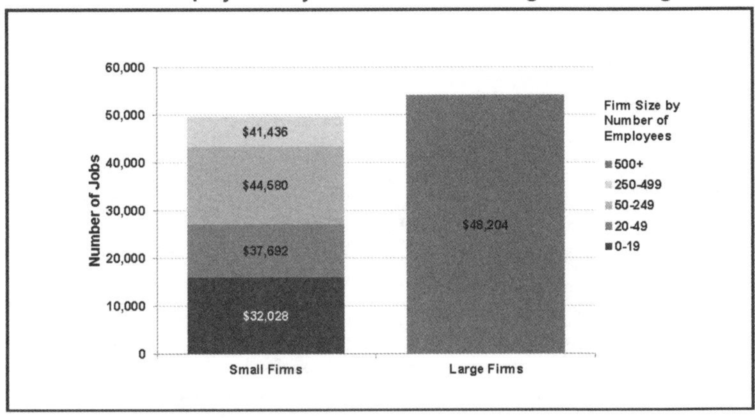


*Sources: **2016 Point-in-Time Data**: American Community Survey. **ALICE Demographics:** American Community Survey; the ALICE Threshold. **Budget:** U.S. Department of Housing and Urban Development; U.S. Department of Agriculture; Bureau of Labor Statistics; Internal Revenue Service; Tax Foundation; and Wisconsin Department of Children and Families, 2016.*

| Outagamie County, 2016 | | |
|---|---|---|
| Town | Total HH | % ALICE & Poverty |
| Appleton city | 23,687 | 37% |
| Bear Creek village | 162 | 43% |
| Black Creek | 506 | 30% |
| Black Creek village | 522 | 33% |
| Bovina | 416 | 19% |
| Buchanan | 2,682 | 17% |
| Center | 1,329 | 17% |
| Cicero | 422 | 32% |
| Combined Locks village | 1,346 | 17% |
| Dale | 1,028 | 15% |
| Deer Creek | 233 | 31% |
| Ellington | 1,084 | 20% |
| Freedom | 2,192 | 23% |
| Grand Chute | 9,781 | 35% |
| Greenville | 3,991 | 14% |
| Hortonia | 407 | 18% |
| Hortonville village | 1,021 | 23% |
| Kaukauna | 435 | 26% |
| Kaukauna city | 6,301 | 34% |
| Kimberly village | 2,807 | 42% |
| Liberty | 316 | 16% |
| Little Chute village | 4,467 | 31% |
| Maine | 330 | 36% |
| Maple Creek | 229 | 32% |
| New London city | 560 | 43% |
| Nichols village | 105 | 54% |
| Oneida | 1,552 | 33% |
| Osborn | 408 | 18% |
| Seymour | 452 | 24% |
| Seymour city | 1,418 | 46% |
| Shiocton village | 370 | 42% |
| Vandenbroek | 566 | 20% |

*Note: Municipal-level data on this page is 5-year averages for Census Places and County Subdivisions. Totals will not always match county-level numbers because some county-level data is 1-year estimates.*

# ALICE IN WINNEBAGO COUNTY

**2016 Point-in-Time Data**

**Population:** 169,886 • **Number of Households:** 69,943
**Median Household Income:** $56,754 (state average: $56,811)
**Unemployment Rate:** 4% (state average: 4.1%)
**ALICE Households:** 21% (state average: 25.8%) • **Households in Poverty:** 11% (state average: 11.7%)

## How has the number of ALICE households changed over time?

**ALICE** is an acronym for **A**sset **L**imited, **I**ncome **C**onstrained, **E**mployed – households that earn more than the Federal Poverty Level, but less than the basic cost of living for the county (the ALICE Threshold). Combined, the number of ALICE and poverty-level households equals the total population struggling to afford basic needs. The number of households below the ALICE Threshold changes over time; households move in and out of poverty and ALICE status as their circumstances improve or worsen. The recovery, which started in 2010, has been uneven across the state. Conditions have improved for some families, but with rising costs, many still find themselves struggling.

### Households by Income, 2010 to 2016

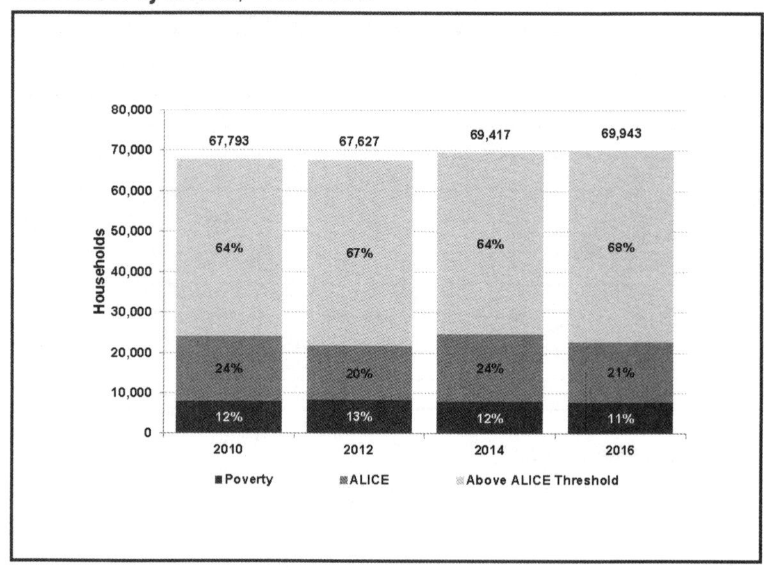


## What types of households are struggling?

The way Americans live is changing. There are more different family and living combinations than ever before, including more adults living alone, with roommates, or with their parents. Families with children are changing: There are more non-married cohabiting parents, same-sex parents, and blended families with remarried parents. The number of senior households is also increasing. Yet all types of households continue to struggle: ALICE and poverty-level households exist across all of these living arrangements.

### Household Types by Income, 2016

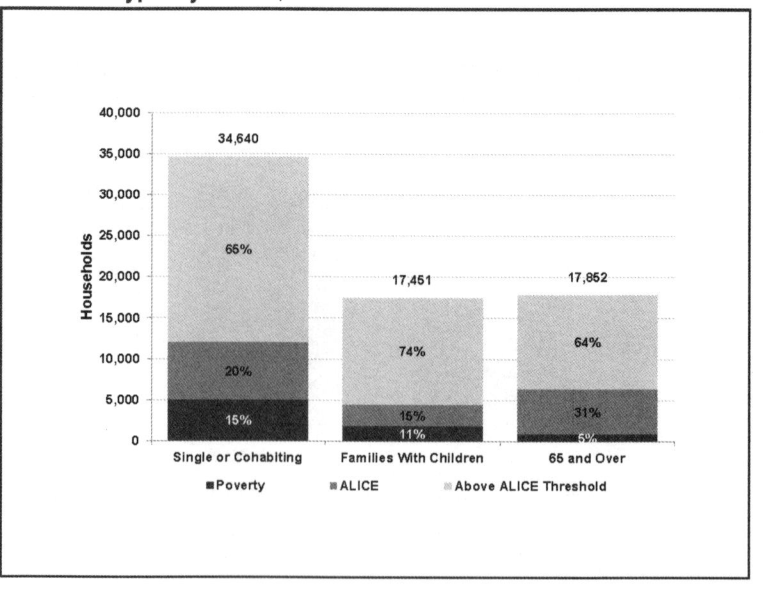

# Why do so many households struggle?

**The cost of living continues to increase...**

The Household Survival Budget reflects the bare minimum that a household needs to live and work today. It does not include savings for emergencies or future goals like college. In 2016, costs were well above the Federal Poverty Level of $11,880 for a single adult and $24,300 for a family of four. Family costs increased by 18 percent statewide from 2010 to 2016, compared to 9 percent inflation nationally.

| Household Survival Budget, Winnebago County | | |
|---|---|---|
| | SINGLE ADULT | 2 ADULTS, 1 INFANT, 1 PRESCHOOLER |
| Monthly Costs | | |
| Housing | $525 | $704 |
| Child Care | $– | $1,398 |
| Food | $158 | $525 |
| Transportation | $349 | $697 |
| Health Care | $214 | $800 |
| Technology | $55 | $75 |
| Miscellaneous | $155 | $486 |
| Taxes | $244 | $656 |
| Monthly Total | $1,700 | $5,341 |
| ANNUAL TOTAL | $20,400 | $64,092 |
| *Hourly Wage* | *$10.20* | *$32.05* |

**...and wages lag behind**

Employment and wages vary by location; firms generally pay higher wages in areas with a higher cost of living, although those wages still do not always cover basic needs. Employment and wages also vary by firm size: Large firms tend to offer higher wages and more job stability; smaller businesses can account for more jobs overall, especially in rural areas, but may pay less and offer less stability. Medium-size firms pay more but typically employ the fewest workers.

## Private-Sector Employment by Firm Size With Average Annual Wages, 2016

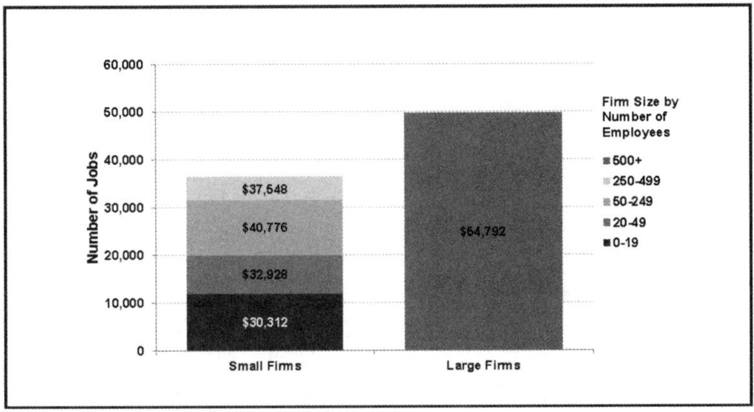


*Sources: **2016 Point-in-Time Data**: American Community Survey. **ALICE Demographics:** American Community Survey; the ALICE Threshold. **Budget:** U.S. Department of Housing and Urban Development; U.S. Department of Agriculture; Bureau of Labor Statistics; Internal Revenue Service; Tax Foundation; and Wisconsin Department of Children and Families, 2016.*

| Winnebago County, 2016 | | |
|---|---|---|
| Town | Total HH | % ALICE & Poverty |
| Algoma | 2,583 | 12% |
| Appleton city | 707 | 58% |
| Black Wolf | 985 | 19% |
| Clayton | 1,496 | 16% |
| Menasha | 8,265 | 34% |
| Menasha city | 6,578 | 42% |
| Neenah | 1,414 | 13% |
| Neenah city | 10,912 | 36% |
| Nekimi | 605 | 27% |
| Nepeuskun | 288 | 24% |
| Omro | 958 | 20% |
| Omro city | 1,372 | 35% |
| Oshkosh | 1,101 | 25% |
| Oshkosh city | 26,294 | 48% |
| Poygan | 545 | 21% |
| Rushford | 667 | 33% |
| Utica | 505 | 17% |
| Vinland | 755 | 18% |
| Winchester | 657 | 16% |
| Winneconne | 945 | 22% |
| Winneconne village | 1,007 | 34% |
| Wolf River | 530 | 27% |

*Note: Municipal-level data on this page is 5-year averages for Census Places and County Subdivisions. Totals will not always match county-level numbers because some county-level data is 1-year estimates.*

# MARKET INSTABILITY

There are a few trends converging to destabilize markets and reshape the American — if not global — workforce: the ripple effects of natural and human-made disasters through a connected global economy, the shifting of risk from companies to workers and from high- to low-wage jobs, and the often disruptive effects of technology on jobs and workplaces.

Each of these trends is likely to become more prevalent going forward, and these changes will impact ALICE workers disproportionately because they have the fewest resources to weather instability and risk. According to a recent workforce survey, more than three-quarters of U.S. workers live paycheck-to-paycheck at least some of the time, and nearly that many are in debt. What makes market instability especially difficult for ALICE families is their lack of financial resilience: They do not have savings or other resources that might sustain them through a low period of income or an unexpected disaster. Instead, an emergency can quickly spiral into a crisis, with devastating consequences for households (CareerBuilder, 2017).

## Disasters Felt Globally

While some Americans may not think much about the global economy, our new economic reality is a complex, integrated system that features both technological advances as well as disruptions. Technology has expanded international connections and increased the speed of these interactions; but that connectedness can function both for better and for worse. When an earthquake and tsunami pummeled Japan in 2011, the global supply chain of semiconductor equipment and materials was disrupted. With Japan responsible for 20 percent of the global semiconductor market, the cost of the world's semiconductor products increased, including those made for Apple's iPad. And there is no global governing body to help moderate the effects of cycles of disaster, inflation, or industry bubbles, as the U.S. has, for example, with the Federal Reserve (World Economic Forum, 2017; van Paasschen, 2017; Morgenstern, 2011; Amadeo, 2011)..

## Workers at Risk

The changing economy has put pressure on businesses to seek new ways to improve productivity and reduce costs. A common practice has been to shift the risk of market fluctuations in supply and demand from the business to the worker. For example, when crops are reduced after a drought, there are lower wages for field hands due to less work even if farm owners can charge more for limited output; and when demand for vacations falls after a hurricane in a tourist destination, hotels and restaurants can cut their losses by sending workers home. Risks from environmental hazards, natural and human-made, are also often pushed onto workers and low-income communities. Lower-income workers are particularly likely to be exposed to hazards such as pollutants in factory work, chemicals and pesticides in farming and manufacturing, and injuries in nursing and construction.

Since these costs are often cumulative, intensifying as the volume of risk increases, years of such practices are being more harshly felt today, such as with the global effects of pollution and climate change. ALICE families are especially vulnerable to events that directly threaten their homes and their jobs: droughts, floods, crop failures, violent weather, rising sea levels, and ocean acidification (van Paasschen, 2017; NASA, 2018).

The growing use of a contingent workforce — another recent structural shift among U.S. businesses — enables companies to scale up or down more nimbly, but it subjects workers to unexpected gains or losses in work hours, making it difficult for ALICE households to pay bills regularly or to make long-term financial plans. Contingent work also reduces the responsibility of employers to provide benefits, such as health insurance and retirement plans. This passes on costs to ALICE families and leaves them more vulnerable should they have a health crisis or have to retire early. And because some employer or government benefits — including paid and unpaid time off, health insurance, unemployment insurance, public assistance, and work supports — are tied to number of hours worked, unpredictable scheduling can put those benefits in jeopardy. For example, low-wage workers are two and a half times more likely to be out of work than other workers, but half as likely to receive unemployment insurance (Garfield, Damico, Stephens, & Rouhani, 2015; Watson, Frohlich, & Johnston, 2014; U.S. Government Accountability Office, 2007).

## Disruptive Technologies and Job Turnover

The cost of disruption is often borne disproportionately by ALICE workers. For example, a technological innovation increases productivity, eliminates some jobs, and creates new ones. The business that invested in the innovation increases profits and the economy benefits from greater productivity. The employee with the new job benefits only if wages are sufficient to cover the cost of training to gain the skills needed for the job, as well as the transaction costs of getting a new job (e.g., job search, relocation, new clothes). The employee in the old job, who may have been excellent in that role, may not have the skills for the new job and/or may be unable to relocate and therefore loses her job, which has huge and immediate costs for herself and her family.

One of the clearest examples of the impact that job turnover has on workers and the economy comes from the North American Free Trade Agreement. Included in the agreement are funds to help workers whose manufacturing jobs move abroad as a result of foreign trade. In 2014, this involved over 62,000 workers, and the cost to help them search for reemployment was just above $300 million, including funds for job training, job search and relocation allowances, income support, and assistance with health care premium costs. That was a cost of more than $4,800 per worker to secure new employment — funds that most ALICE workers who lose their jobs do not have (U.S. Department of Labor, 2014).

Turnover is also costly for businesses. From a human-resources perspective, experts estimates that turnover costs account for 20 to 30 percent of the annual salary of workers making less than $50,000, a cost that includes recruiting, interviewing, hiring, orientation and training, lost productivity, potential customer dissatisfaction, reduced or lost business, administrative costs, and lost expertise (Boushey & Glynn, 2012; Merhar, 2016; Bersin, 2013; Bolden-Barrett, 2017).

Finally, there are the costs of disruptive technologies to consumers, including the time it takes to learn about a new product or process, the actual cost of the item, cancellation fees, and the time and effort to implement and incorporate it into their lives. ALICE families especially do not have the time or funds to adapt, and the ongoing stress of insufficient income is exacerbated by their inability to upgrade to new technologies that ostensibly make everyday life easier (Klemperer, 1987; Zhang, Chen, Zhao, & Yao, 2014).

## Future Jobs

Wisconsin's workforce faces a future dominated by low-paying jobs requiring few advanced educational credentials. From 2018 to 2025, three-quarters of the fastest-growing jobs in Wisconsin will pay less than $20 per hour. In terms of education, only 19 percent of new jobs will require a bachelor's degree, and only 13 percent will require some college or post-secondary non-degree award. More than half of new jobs (54 percent) will not require a formal educational credential at all, and another 15 percent will require only a high school diploma (Projections Central, 2016; Bureau of Labor Statistics, 2016; Wisconsin Department of Workforce Development, 2018) (Figure 40).

Furthermore, many of these jobs are also at the greatest risk of being replaced by technology. Three-quarters (76 percent) of jobs in Wisconsin's top-20 fastest-growing occupations could be replaced by technology in the next two decades. In addition to automating existing jobs, technology is creating new on-demand jobs and services, with the most attention going to gig-economy jobs such as TaskRabbit work and Uber and Lyft driving (Frey & Osborne, September 2013).

**Predicting new occupations:** Moving beyond TaskRabbit and Uber, there are a wide array of new jobs predicted to arise in the next 20 to 30 years, including augmented reality architects, alternative currency bankers, waste data managers, 3-D printing engineers, privacy managers, wind-turbine repair techs, nano-medics, drone dispatchers, robotic earthworm drivers, body part and limb makers, memory augmentation therapists, mass-energy-storage developers, and self-driving-car mechanics (Frey T. , 2011; Mejia, 2017; World Economic Forum, 2016; Hagan, 2017).

While these jobs seem a long way from today's mechanics and personal care providers, most are still maintainer jobs, largely filled by ALICE workers who care for the infrastructure and the workforce, in occupations that ensure the economy runs smoothly. In other words, our physical infrastructure may change, but it will still need maintenance, and the maintainer workforce will still need to be educated and cared for (Vinsel & Russell, 2016).

The new jobs, however, will not necessarily be filled by the same workers who held the jobs that these new titles replace. For example, a cashier does not necessarily have the skills to repair digital-checkout kiosks. Jobs that remain, especially those that require lower levels of education, will be service jobs that cannot be automated and will continue to be the lowest-paid, such as health aides, janitors, sales representatives, and movers. Yet even these jobs will increasingly require digital skills (Brynjolfsson & McAfee, 2014; Frey & Osborne, September 2013).

**Ability to work with technology:** In the face of rapidly rising computing power, an ability to work with data and make data-based decisions will become an increasingly vital skill even within maintainer jobs, so ALICE workers will need new skill sets. The ability to work with technology will be increasingly important for jobs at all levels, from retail assistants to more senior positions. With the increasing amount of digital information being generated and stored, there will be more value placed on utilizing data to improve business productivity. And with increased mechanization, many jobs will require working alongside machines as well as building and repairing them. In Wisconsin, this dynamic is already a big part of agriculture and manufacturing.

The McKinsey Global Institute estimates that in 60 percent of all occupations, an average of 30 percent of work activities are automatable, and therefore more workers will be required to work alongside machines (Manyika J. , 2017). For example, at Ford's Chicago Assembly Plant, operators used to spend 70 percent of their time scanning and 30 percent repairing defects. Now they spend 10 percent of their time scanning and 90 percent of their time finessing the final assembly of a vehicle (Pete, 2013) (Hagan, 2017).

In addition, the pace of these changes may have to be faster than anticipated. By one estimate, 50 percent of subject knowledge acquired during the first year of a four-year technical degree in 2016 will be outdated by the time students graduate (World Economic Forum, 2016; Organisation for Economic Co-operation and Development, 2016; Carnevale, Smith, Gullish, & Hanson, 2015).

**More consultants, more risk:** Initially, the gig economy was seen as a way for many ALICE households to fill short-term gaps in standard employment, with work that might be more lucrative than jobs in the traditional employment market. However, the size of the contingent workforce has increased to up to one-third of the overall workforce, with estimates that it could reach 40 to 50 percent by 2020. With more and more workers solely reliant on contract work, the number of people experiencing gaps in income and going without benefits is also rising, and this trend is expected to increase (Gaggl & Eden, 2015; Abraham, Haltiwanger, Sandusky, & Spletzer, 2016; Katz & Krueger, 2016; Freelancers Union & Elance-oDesk, 2016; U.S. Government Accountability Office, 2015; Edison Research, 2018; Smith, 2016; Manyika, et al., 2016; Intuit, 2017).

**Figure 40.**
**New Job Growth by Occupation, Wisconsin, 2017 to 2025**

* *Percent of current jobs changed, disrupted or eliminated by technology*

| Occupation | 2017 Employment | Annual New Growth | Hourly Wage | Education or Training | Likelihood of Being Replaced by Tech |
|---|---|---|---|---|---|
| Retail Salespersons | 89,387 | 290 | $10.27 | None | 74% |
| Food Prep, Including Fast Food | 63,141 | 861 | $9.05 | None | 92% |
| Personal Care Aides | 62,452 | 1,793 | $10.74 | None | 79% |
| Customer Service Representatives | 57,816 | 462 | $16.99 | High school diploma or equivalent | 1% |
| Registered Nurses | 56,212 | 533 | $32.58 | Bachelor's degree | 85% |
| Laborers and Movers, Hand | 55,335 | 271 | $13.99 | None | 55% |
| Heavy and Tractor-Trailer Truck Drivers | 52,132 | 687 | $19.61 | Postsecondary non-degree award | 6% |
| Janitors and Cleaners | 49,003 | 395 | $11.54 | None | 6% |
| Waiters and Waitresses | 43,448 | 233 | $9.17 | None | 66% |
| Sales Representatives | 40,562 | 474 | $28.69 | High school diploma or equivalent | 96% |
| General and Operations Managers | 35,434 | 282 | $44.15 | Bachelor's degree | 92% |
| Nursing Assistants | 34,239 | 458 | $13.47 | Postsecondary non-degree award | 16% |
| First-Line Supervisors of Office and Administrative Support Workers | 29,254 | 214 | $24.84 | High school diploma or equivalent | 85% |
| Bartenders | 26,732 | 266 | $9.23 | None | 77% |
| Maids and Housekeeping Cleaners | 26,284 | 217 | $10.09 | None | 94% |
| Accountants and Auditors | 23,026 | 264 | $30.86 | Bachelor's degree | 95% |
| Landscaping and Groundskeeping Workers | 21,242 | 239 | $12.62 | None | 94% |
| Cooks, Restaurant | 19,639 | 338 | $11.19 | None | 86% |
| Computer Systems Analysts | 14,628 | 405 | $36.46 | Bachelor's degree | 61% |
| Market Research Analysts and Marketing Specialists | 11,571 | 219 | $25.63 | Bachelor's degree | 69% |
| Computer-Controlled Machine Tool Operators | 10,751 | 229 | $19.15 | High school diploma or equivalent | 1% |

*Source: Frey & Osborne, September 2013; Wisconsin Department of Workforce Development, 2018*

## Appendex — Selected Reports

# Examining Job Automation in Wisconsin's Workforce

Ryan Long
Reginal Economist,
Department of Workforce Develoment

## Propensity for Automation by Typical Educational Requirements

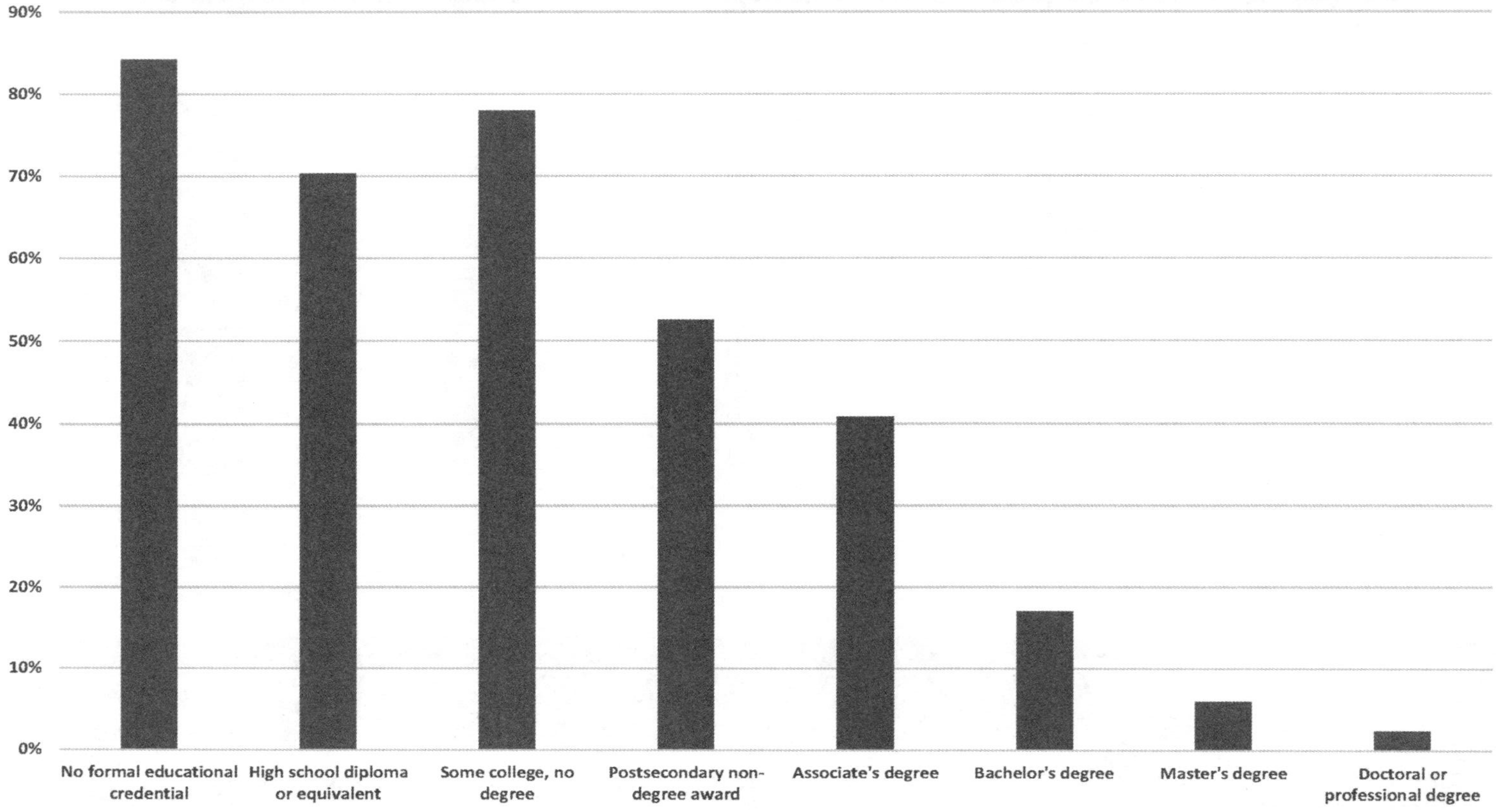

DWD

90%
80%
70%
60%
50%
40%
30%
20%
10%
0%

No formal educational credential
High school diploma or equivalent
Some college, no degree
Postsecondary non-degree award
Associate's degree
Bachelor's degree
Master's degree
Doctoral or professional degree

**Source**: The Future of Employment: How Susceptible are Jobs to Computerisation, C.B. Frey and M.A. Osborne, September 17, 2013, Oxford Martin School, University of Oxford; OES.

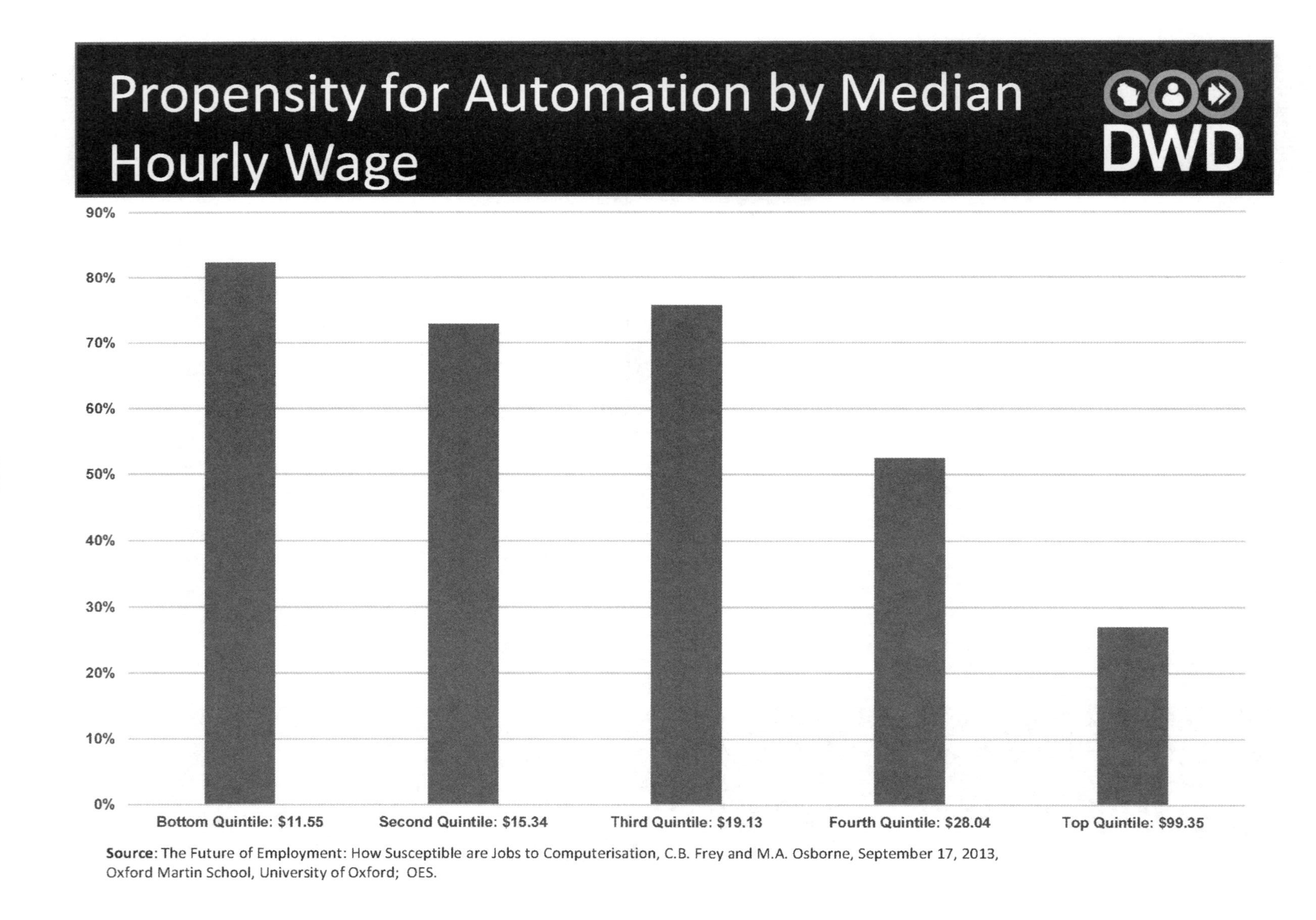
Propensity for Automation by Median Hourly Wage
DWD
90%
80%
70%
60%
50%
40%
30%
20%
10%
0%
Bottom Quintile: $11.55
Second Quintile: $15.34
Third Quintile: $19.13
Fourth Quintile: $28.04
Top Quintile: $99.35
**Source**: The Future of Employment: How Susceptible are Jobs to Computerisation, C.B. Frey and M.A. Osborne, September 17, 2013, Oxford Martin School, University of Oxford; OES.

Appendex — Selected Reports

## The State of America's Children: 2017

Children's Defense Fund

# THE STATE OF AMERICA'S CHILDREN® 2017

Despite seven years of economic recovery and a recent decline in child poverty for all racial/ethnic groups, children remain the poorest age group in America. Nearly 1 in 5 lived in poverty in 2016 (18 percent)—more than 13.2 million children—a poverty rate one-and-a-half times higher than that for adults ages 18-64 (12 percent) and two times higher than that for adults 65 and older (9 percent) (see **Table 2**). Children are considered poor if they live in a family of four with an annual income below $24,563, which amounts to $2,047 a month, $472 a week, or $68 a day (see **Table 3**). But about 3 million children in the U.S. are living in families trying to survive on $2 a day for each family member, which rivals child poverty in some of the world's poorest countries and should be a call to action for us all.[1]

Child poverty is related to both age and race/ethnicity. The youngest children are the poorest and nearly 70 percent of poor children in America are children of color.

- Nearly 1 in 5 children under 6 were poor and almost half of them lived in extreme poverty (see **Table 4**).
- About 1 in 3 Black (31 percent) and American Indian/Alaska Native children (31 percent) and 1 in 4 Hispanic children (27 percent) were poor compared with 1 in 9 White children (11 percent) (see **Tables 5-6**).

Children's chances of being poor are also partly a result of the lottery of geography.

- More than 25 percent of Black children were poor in 37 states and the District of Columbia in 2016; Hispanic children, in 34 states; and American Indian/Native Alaska children, in 29 states.
- Only two states had White child poverty rates higher than 20 percent (see **Table 6**).

The toxic stress of early poverty stunts children's development, creating opportunity gaps than can last a lifetime and harm the nation's economy.

- Poor children are more likely to have poor academic achievement, drop out of high school and later become unemployed, experience economic hardship and be involved in the criminal justice system. Children who experience poverty are also more likely to be poor at age 30 than children who never experience poverty.[2]
- Lost productivity, worsened health and increased crime stemming from child poverty cost the nation about $500 billion dollars a year.[3]

Children's Defense Fund

## Nearly 1 in 5 children were poor in 2016. Nearly 70 percent of them were children of color and 2 in 3 lived with at least one working family member.

### Table 2: Poor Children in America in 2016—A Portrait

| | Number Who Are Poor | Percent Who Are Poor | Percent of Poor Children |
|---|---|---|---|
| **Among All Children** | 13,253,000 | 18.0% | 100.0% |
| **Extremely Poor** | 6,027,000 | 8.2 | 45.5 |
| **Under 6** | 4,674,000 | 19.7 | 35.3 |
| **Under 6 and Extremely Poor** | 2,271,000 | 9.6 | 17.1 |
| **By Race/Ethnicity** | | | |
| White, Non-Hispanic | 4,050,000 | 10.8 | 27.9 |
| Hispanic | 4,890,000 | 26.6 | 33.7 |
| Black | 3,418,000 | 30.8 | 23.6 |
| Asian | 393,000 | 10.6 | 2.7 |
| American Indian/Alaska Native | 193,000 | 31.0 | 1.3 |
| Native Hawaiian/Other Pacific Islander | 66,000 | 24.5 | 0.5 |
| Two or More Races | 527,000 | 17.8 | 3.6 |
| **By Geography** | | | |
| In Cities > 50,000 | 5,377,000 | 23.1 | 40.6 |
| In Suburbs | 5,588,000 | 13.8 | 42.2 |
| Outside Cities and Suburbs | 2,288,000 | 23.1 | 17.3 |
| **By Region** | | | |
| Northeast | 1,829,000 | 15.6 | 13.8 |
| Midwest | 2,696,000 | 17.3 | 20.3 |
| South | 5,696,000 | 20.0 | 43.0 |
| West | 3,031,000 | 17.0 | 22.9 |
| **Among Children Related to Head of Household** | 12,803,000 | 17.6 | 100.0 |
| **By Family Structure** | | | |
| In Single-Parent Family | 8,664,000 | 37.2 | 67.7 |
| In Married-Couple Family | 4,178,000 | 8.4 | 32.6 |
| **By Family Working Status** | | | |
| Any Family Member Works | 8,900,000 | 13.1 | 63.6 |
| Works Full-Time, Year-Round | 3,957,000 | 6.8 | 28.3 |
| Head of Family Works | 6,911,000 | 11.9 | 49.4 |
| Works Full-Time, Year-Round | 2,720,000 | 6.3 | 19.4 |
| **Adults 18-64** | 22,795,000 | 11.6 | |
| **Seniors 65+** | 4,568,000 | 9.3 | |

Notes: A family of four was considered poor in 2016 with an annual income below $24,563 and extremely poor with an income below half that amount ($12,282). Poverty estimates differ based on the source of the Census data. Census data on poverty is collected through both the American Community Survey (ACS) and Current Population Survey (CPS). The CPS provides the most accurate national data on poverty and is therefore the official source of national poverty estimates. The ACS uses a larger sample size and is preferred for state-level poverty data.

Sources: U.S. Census Bureau, Current Population Survey. 2017. "2016 Annual Social and Economic Supplement," Tables POV01, POV03, POV13, POV21, POV40, and 3.

Public education has been a crucial pathway out of poverty for families for generations, offering children opportunities to gain the social, economic, cultural and political capital necessary to realize their full potential, support their future families and give back to society. However, with fewer high-quality early childhood opportunities, poor children and children of color often begin school behind their peers. With inequitable resources, including less access to high-quality teachers and programming, they continue to fall further behind as they age.

- Less than half of poor children are ready for school at age 5 compared with 75 percent of their wealthier peers.[1]
- More than 75 percent of lower-income fourth and eighth grade public school students could not read or compute at grade level in 2015 compared with less than 55 percent of higher-income students (see **Table 21**).
- More than 73 percent of fourth and eighth grade Black and Hispanic public school students could not read or compute at grade level in 2015 compared with less than 60 percent of White students (see **Tables 22-23**).
- Less than 80 percent of Black, Hispanic and American Indian/Alaska Native public school students graduated on time during the 2014-2015 school year compared with 87 percent of White students (see **Table 24**).

Hostile school climates and exclusionary discipline practices disproportionately deny children of color the opportunity for success and contribute to the school-to-prison pipeline.

- During the 2011-2012 school year, the suspension rate for Black students in public elementary school was more than five times that for White students (see **Table 25**).
- The suspension rate for Black students in public secondary school was more than three times that for White students (see **Table 26**).

In 2015, the percent of lower-income fourth and eighth grade public school students performing below grade level in reading and math was almost two times that of higher-income students.

**Table 21: Percent of Fourth and Eighth Grade Public School Students Performing below Grade Level in Reading and Math by Income Status, 2015**

| | Lower-Income Students | | | | Higher-Income Students | | | |
|---|---|---|---|---|---|---|---|---|
| | 4th Grade | | 8th Grade | | 4th Grade | | 8th Grade | |
| | Reading | Math | Reading | Math | Reading | Math | Reading | Math |
| Alabama | 81% | 85% | 83% | 93% | 55% | 57% | 63% | 71% |
| Alaska | 83 | 79 | 83 | 82 | 57 | 50 | 56 | 55 |
| Arizona | 83 | 75 | 79 | 77 | 48 | 42 | 57 | 50 |
| Arkansas | 76 | 75 | 83 | 84 | 52 | 54 | 58 | 62 |
| California | 84 | 84 | 82 | 84 | 52 | 49 | 57 | 55 |
| Colorado | 79 | 75 | 80 | 81 | 46 | 41 | 48 | 48 |
| Connecticut | 80 | 83 | 77 | 87 | 43 | 45 | 46 | 52 |
| Delaware | 79 | 77 | 81 | 84 | 52 | 54 | 61 | 61 |
| District of Columbia | 86 | 82 | 90 | 89 | 34 | 31 | 54 | 54 |
| Florida | 71 | 69 | 78 | 84 | 45 | 40 | 55 | 56 |
| Georgia | 77 | 77 | 80 | 85 | 45 | 44 | 54 | 48 |
| Hawaii | 83 | 74 | 84 | 80 | 57 | 47 | 65 | 59 |
| Idaho | 76 | 74 | 73 | 79 | 51 | 48 | 54 | 55 |
| Illinois | 80 | 79 | 78 | 82 | 45 | 44 | 51 | 53 |
| Indiana | 72 | 64 | 77 | 76 | 48 | 35 | 49 | 49 |
| Iowa | 77 | 73 | 78 | 80 | 51 | 43 | 56 | 53 |
| Kansas | 80 | 73 | 78 | 81 | 46 | 42 | 53 | 54 |
| Kentucky | 71 | 71 | 74 | 83 | 43 | 41 | 51 | 59 |
| Louisiana | 79 | 79 | 84 | 90 | 56 | 51 | 64 | 67 |
| Maine | 77 | 73 | 76 | 77 | 52 | 45 | 56 | 55 |
| Maryland | 82 | 79 | 81 | 85 | 48 | 43 | 49 | 52 |
| Massachusetts | 71 | 69 | 72 | 69 | 35 | 29 | 41 | 34 |

| | | | | | | | | |
|---|---|---|---|---|---|---|---|---|
| Michigan | 84 | 83 | 82 | 86 | 60 | 51 | 57 | 59 |
| Minnesota | 80 | 67 | 78 | 73 | 48 | 33 | 51 | 41 |
| Mississippi | 81 | 79 | 87 | 86 | 55 | 48 | 61 | 58 |
| Missouri | 75 | 74 | 78 | 84 | 50 | 47 | 51 | 55 |
| Montana | 76 | 73 | 77 | 74 | 51 | 47 | 53 | 52 |
| Nebraska | 77 | 73 | 78 | 80 | 45 | 39 | 50 | 50 |
| Nevada | 80 | 79 | 83 | 85 | 58 | 51 | 61 | 61 |
| New Hampshire | 74 | 69 | 73 | 75 | 46 | 40 | 49 | 47 |
| New Jersey | 79 | 75 | 81 | 78 | 43 | 38 | 49 | 42 |
| New Mexico | 83 | 80 | 86 | 86 | 60 | 54 | 67 | 62 |
| New York | 79 | 77 | 78 | 79 | 47 | 49 | 54 | 56 |
| North Carolina | 75 | 70 | 82 | 81 | 41 | 33 | 52 | 48 |
| North Dakota | 77 | 74 | 82 | 78 | 56 | 46 | 60 | 53 |
| Ohio | 77 | 76 | 80 | 80 | 48 | 36 | 50 | 51 |
| Oklahoma | 77 | 75 | 79 | 87 | 52 | 44 | 60 | 65 |
| Oregon | 77 | 73 | 76 | 79 | 48 | 46 | 51 | 50 |
| Pennsylvania | 76 | 76 | 80 | 82 | 45 | 39 | 45 | 48 |
| Rhode Island | 76 | 79 | 81 | 85 | 46 | 48 | 52 | 54 |
| South Carolina | 79 | 76 | 83 | 86 | 47 | 43 | 57 | 59 |
| South Dakota | 80 | 75 | 77 | 81 | 55 | 49 | 59 | 58 |
| Tennessee | 78 | 73 | 80 | 83 | 50 | 42 | 52 | 56 |
| Texas | 80 | 70 | 82 | 80 | 51 | 32 | 60 | 53 |
| Utah | 73 | 72 | 78 | 78 | 52 | 48 | 53 | 54 |
| Vermont | 70 | 73 | 71 | 73 | 45 | 45 | 47 | 48 |
| Virginia | 78 | 73 | 83 | 83 | 42 | 38 | 52 | 50 |
| Washington | 77 | 71 | 78 | 76 | 42 | 34 | 48 | 45 |
| West Virginia | 75 | 74 | 78 | 85 | 56 | 50 | 64 | 69 |
| Wisconsin | 81 | 74 | 79 | 81 | 50 | 40 | 53 | 48 |
| Wyoming | 72 | 66 | 78 | 80 | 51 | 42 | 56 | 56 |
| **United States** | **79%** | **76%** | **80%** | **82%** | **48%** | **42%** | **53%** | **52%** |

Notes: Lower-income students are students who qualify for free and reduced-price school lunch, which means their families' incomes are at or below 185 percent of the Federal Poverty Level (FPL). Higher-income students are students who do not qualify, or whose families' incomes are higher than 185 percent of the FPL. "Below grade level" means below proficient.

Source: U.S. Department of Education. 2016. "2015 Mathematics and Reading Assessments Report Card: Summary Data Tables with Additional Detail for Average Scores and Achievement Levels for States and Jurisdictions." https://www.nationsreportcard.gov/reading_math_2015/#reading/scores?grade=4.

## The U.S. spent more than two times as much per prisoner as per public school student during 2011–2012.

### Table 27: Public Spending on Prisoners vs. Public School Students, 2011-2012

| | Spending per Prisoner | Spending per Public School Student | Ratio of Spending per Prisoner vs. Public School Student | Rank by Ratio[a] |
|---|---|---|---|---|
| Alabama | $16,511 | $8,577 | 1.9 | 4 |
| Alaska | 40,461 | 17,475 | 2.3 | 17 |
| Arizona | 19,246 | 7,382 | 2.6 | 23 |
| Arkansas | 22,838 | 9,536 | 2.4 | 18 |
| California | 49,283 | 9,329 | 5.3 | 49 |
| Colorado | 29,339 | 8,594 | 3.4 | 37 |
| Connecticut | 38,532 | 16,855 | 2.3 | 16 |
| Delaware | 33,316 | 13,580 | 2.5 | 20 |
| District of Columbia[b] | n/a | 19,847 | n/a | – |
| Florida | 17,004 | 8,520 | 2.0 | 6 |
| Georgia | 18,018 | 9,272 | 1.9 | 5 |
| Hawaii | 36,359 | 11,973 | 3.0 | 30 |
| Idaho | 23,549 | 6,626 | 3.6 | 41 |
| Illinois | 23,973 | 12,011 | 2.0 | 7 |
| Indiana | 21,045 | 9,588 | 2.2 | 12 |
| Iowa | 29,014 | 10,027 | 2.9 | 28 |
| Kansas | 26,467 | 10,021 | 2.6 | 24 |
| Kentucky | 34,030 | 9,327 | 3.6 | 42 |
| Louisiana | 22,500 | 10,726 | 2.1 | 9 |
| Maine | 41,062 | 12,335 | 3.3 | 35 |
| Maryland | 47,618 | 13,871 | 3.4 | 38 |
| Massachusetts | 77,898 | 14,844 | 5.2 | 48 |
| Michigan | 30,411 | 10,477 | 2.9 | 29 |
| Minnesota | 29,677 | 10,781 | 2.8 | 26 |

| | | | | |
|---|---|---|---|---|
| Mississippi | 17,519 | 8,097 | 2.2 | 11 |
| Missouri | 19,146 | 9,514 | 2.0 | 8 |
| Montana | 46,325 | 10,569 | 4.4 | 45 |
| Nebraska | 21,977 | 11,640 | 1.9 | 3 |
| Nevada | 17,254 | 8,130 | 2.1 | 10 |
| New Hampshire | 31,303 | 13,774 | 2.3 | 14 |
| New Jersey | 44,512 | 17,982 | 2.5 | 22 |
| New Mexico | 40,124 | 9,013 | 4.5 | 46 |
| New York | 44,232 | 19,396 | 2.3 | 15 |
| North Carolina | 28,833 | 8,160 | 3.5 | 40 |
| North Dakota | 51,853 | 11,246 | 4.6 | 47 |
| Ohio | 20,003 | 11,323 | 1.8 | 2 |
| Oklahoma | 18,732 | 7,763 | 2.4 | 19 |
| Oregon | 32,728 | 9,485 | 3.5 | 39 |
| Pennsylvania | 34,710 | 13,091 | 2.7 | 25 |
| Rhode Island | 48,579 | 15,172 | 3.2 | 33 |
| South Carolina | 20,390 | 9,077 | 2.2 | 13 |
| South Dakota | 26,404 | 8,593 | 3.1 | 31 |
| Tennessee | 26,658 | 8,354 | 3.2 | 32 |
| Texas | 20,177 | 8,213 | 2.5 | 21 |
| Utah | 35,206 | 6,441 | 5.5 | 50 |
| Vermont | 28,894 | 16,651 | 1.7 | 1 |
| Virginia | 30,424 | 10,656 | 2.9 | 27 |
| Washington | 36,997 | 9,617 | 3.8 | 43 |
| West Virginia | 46,218 | 11,579 | 4.0 | 44 |
| Wisconsin | 36,382 | 11,233 | 3.2 | 34 |
| Wyoming | 53,339 | 15,988 | 3.3 | 36 |
| **United States** | **$24,836** | **$10,667** | **2.3** | |

[a]States are ranked 1-50 from lowest to highest ratio of spending per prisoner vs. public school student.

[b]"n/a" means data were not available because the District of Columbia does not have a prison system.

Sources: Carson, E. Ann and Joseph Mulako-Wangota. 2015. "Count of Total Custody Population (Including Private Prisons; Only 1999-Present)." Bureau of Justice Statistics. https://www.bjs.gov/; U.S. Department of Education. 2014. "National Public Education Financial Survey," Table 236.65. http://nces.ed.gov/programs/digest/d14/tables/dt14_236.65.asp.

## How America Ranks among 35 Rich (OECD) Countries for Investing in Children and Key Child Outcomes

The U.S. is one of the richest countries in the world having the highest gross domestic product among member countries of the Organisation for Economic Co-operation and Development (OECD) and the most billionaires. The U.S. also has the largest budget as the federal government spends more than any other country. Unfortunately, we do not prioritize our children in that budget. We spend more money than any other country on defense but invest less in areas such as early childhood and education. In turn, our children are far behind on key performance outcomes. Income inequality in the U.S. is also high, such that few are rich and many of our children are poor. Below, we have included key facts regarding how America ranks among 35 rich countries for investing in children and on key child outcomes. For all measures, countries were ranked 1-35 with one meaning a country is doing the best and 35 meaning a country is doing the worst. For some measures, data were not available for all 35 countries.

**America's Rank for Income and Wealth**

- 1st for gross domestic product (purchasing power parity), 2016[1]
- 1st for number of billionaires, 2017[2]
- 32nd for income inequality, meaning the U.S. has one of the largest gaps between the rich and poor, 2015[3]

**America's Rank for Government Spending**

- 1st for military spending (in US dollars), 2016[4]
- 2nd for military spending (percent of GDP), 2016[5]
- 8th for spending on health (percent of GDP), 2016[6]
- 30th for spending on early childhood education and care (percent of GDP), 2013[7]
- 20th for spending on education (percent of GDP), 2013[8]

**America's Rank on Key Child Outcomes**

- 30th for percent of children in poverty, 2015[9]
- 33rd for percent of children under age 15 who do not have adequate access to food, 2014/2015[10]
- 30th for percent of infants born weighing less than 5.5 pounds (low birthweight), 2014[11]
- 26th for percent of 1-year-olds vaccinated for diphtheria, tetanus and pertussis, 2014[12]
- 32nd for number of infants who die before their 1st birthday, 2014[13]
- 31st for number of teenage births, 2015[14]
- 29th for percent of children under age 5 enrolled in early childhood and primary education, 2014[15]
- 20th for reading scores of 15-year-olds, 2015[16]
- 31st for math scores of 15-year-olds, 2015[17]

Among rich countries, the U.S. also has the highest number of children and teens killed with guns and is the only member of the United Nations (U.N.) that has not ratified the U.N. Convention on the Rights of the Child.[18]

Childhood should be a time of growth and positive development in caring families and communities. However, far too many children—particularly those who are poor; children of color; children with disabilities; children with mental health and substance abuse challenges; children subjected to neglect, abuse and/or other violence; children in foster care; and lesbian, gay, bisexual, transgender, and queer (LGBTQ) children—are pushed out of homes and schools into the streets and the juvenile justice and/or adult criminal justice systems. An increasing number of girls are also being subjected to what many call the "sexual abuse to prison pipeline."[1] These children are at the heart of Children's Defense Fund's Cradle to Prison Pipeline® campaign, which works to end the criminalization of children in America.

- In 2014 more than 1 million children were arrested in the U.S. In six states more than 5 percent of children were arrested (see **Table 34**).
- Sixty-three percent of children arrested in the U.S. were White and 34 percent were Black.[2] However, Black children were approximately two-and-a-half times more likely to be arrested than White children.[3] Children of color were more likely to be formally processed and locked in facilities instead of connected to a community-based program.
- Overall, youth incarceration has continued to decrease in recent years. In 2015, 48,043 children and youths were held in residential placement on an average night in the U.S.[4] However, children of color had a greater percent of residential placements than White children, and Black children had the highest percent. Of those incarcerated, 69 percent were children of color: 42 percent were Black and 22 percent were Hispanic. Moreover, 85 percent were male (see **Table 35**).
- During 1992-2013, the share of girls involved in the juvenile justice system increased at least 40 percent at every decision point, including arrests, detentions, court caseloads and post-adjudication placements.[5]
- In 2015 the ratio of the residential placement rate for girls of color to that for White girls was 2 to 1 nationally, and in 30 states and the District of Columbia, the placement rate for non-Hispanic Black girls exceeded the rate for all other racial/ethnic groups.[6]

## As of 2016, nearly half of all children have had at least one Adverse Childhood Experience (ACE) and 1 in 5 have had at least two ACEs.

### Table 33: Percent of Children Who Have Had Adverse Childhood Experiences (ACEs) by Number and Type of ACE, 2016

| | Number of ACEs: | | | Type of ACE: | | | | | | | | |
|---|---|---|---|---|---|---|---|---|---|---|---|---|
| | Percent With 0 ACES | Percent With 1 ACE | Percent With 2+ ACES | Hard to Get by on Family's Income | Parent Divorced or Separated | Parent Died | Parent Served Time in Jail | Witnessed Domestic Violence | Victim or Witness of Neigh-borhood Violence | Lived With Anyone Mentally Ill, Suicidal or Depressed | Lived With Anyone With Alcohol or Drug Problem | Treated or Judged Unfairly Due to Race/ Ethnicity |
| Alabama | 49.9% | 22.4% | 27.7% | 27.7% | 29.9% | 4.8% | 7.6% | 6.2% | 4.1% | 7.6% | 10.1% | 3.5% |
| Alaska | 55.7 | 20.6 | 23.8 | 22.0 | 27.4 | 3.8 | 8.8 | 6.7 | 4.5 | 10.5 | 13.4 | 3.3 |
| Arizona | 50.6 | 18.8 | 30.6 | 26.9 | 31.9 | 2.8 | 12.9 | 10.8 | 5.9 | 9.9 | 15.9 | 3.9 |
| Arkansas | 44.1 | 26.2 | 29.6 | 31.5 | 33.3 | 5.9 | 16.0 | 9.7 | 5.0 | 10.2 | 11.6 | 3.7 |
| California | 57.9 | 25.7 | 16.4 | 22.0 | 21.6 | 1.5 | 5.8 | 2.9 | 2.0 | 5.6 | 7.3 | 4.0 |
| Colorado | 53.7 | 24.0 | 22.3 | 23.2 | 26.6 | 2.5 | 7.8 | 5.4 | 3.4 | 8.7 | 12.2 | 4.7 |
| Connecticut | 57.8 | 22.8 | 19.4 | 24.5 | 25.0 | 2.5 | 6.0 | 4.4 | 3.7 | 7.7 | 7.9 | 3.0 |
| Delaware | 51.7 | 25.7 | 22.6 | 23.8 | 24.9 | 3.4 | 10.4 | 6.7 | 5.7 | 7.4 | 7.9 | 3.4 |
| District of Columbia | 52.9 | 25.3 | 21.8 | 21.4 | 25.4 | 4.6 | 9.2 | 5.6 | 9.4 | 5.3 | 6.9 | 3.2 |
| Florida | 48.0 | 27.2 | 24.8 | 26.9 | 30.4 | 4.4 | 11.1 | 6.8 | 4.7 | 5.5 | 7.9 | 4.0 |
| Georgia | 52.3 | 22.7 | 25.0 | 26.5 | 27.3 | 6.2 | 10.1 | 5.5 | 6.2 | 9.2 | 8.5 | 5.0 |
| Hawaii | 56.8 | 21.8 | 21.4 | 24.4 | 22.0 | 1.8 | 4.9 | 9.6 | 7.1 | 4.6 | 10.0 | 2.2 |
| Idaho | 49.1 | 27.5 | 23.4 | 28.8 | 25.6 | 3.4 | 9.3 | 5.9 | 4.2 | 13.4 | 11.2 | 1.9 |
| Illinois | 60.3 | 20.3 | 19.5 | 23.5 | 19.3 | 3.1 | 6.1 | 5.8 | 4.3 | 7.9 | 7.7 | 4.9 |
| Indiana | 52.7 | 23.1 | 24.2 | 23.6 | 27.4 | 5.3 | 10.4 | 7.5 | 5.9 | 9.2 | 9.6 | 4.1 |
| Iowa | 56.2 | 23.8 | 20.0 | 24.6 | 22.9 | 2.2 | 5.9 | 5.2 | 5.3 | 9.6 | 9.4 | 3.0 |
| Kansas | 54.8 | 23.4 | 21.7 | 22.9 | 27.3 | 2.4 | 9.4 | 6.1 | 3.6 | 8.6 | 10.9 | 1.6 |
| Kentucky | 46.9 | 26.3 | 26.9 | 26.7 | 32.8 | 2.7 | 14.9 | 6.8 | 3.3 | 9.9 | 12.0 | 2.3 |
| Louisiana | 46.3 | 25.4 | 28.2 | 29.6 | 30.2 | 5.5 | 14.4 | 5.7 | 4.7 | 7.8 | 10.4 | 4.8 |
| Maine | 48.3 | 27.1 | 24.6 | 30.6 | 30.2 | 2.2 | 6.1 | 8.0 | 5.8 | 13.9 | 11.0 | 2.3 |
| Maryland | 59.0 | 25.6 | 15.4 | 21.5 | 18.1 | 3.2 | 3.9 | 4.0 | 2.2 | 5.4 | 6.3 | 4.0 |
| Massachusetts | 61.2 | 22.9 | 15.9 | 22.8 | 19.1 | 3.8 | 3.5 | 2.8 | 2.4 | 6.6 | 6.2 | 1.6 |
| Michigan | 53.8 | 24.4 | 21.8 | 22.8 | 24.8 | 4.5 | 6.4 | 5.5 | 4.9 | 7.6 | 7.4 | 4.9 |

| | | | | | | | | | | | | |
|---|---|---|---|---|---|---|---|---|---|---|---|---|
| Minnesota | 61.9 | 21.3 | 16.8 | 20.7 | 20.1 | 2.1 | 6.5 | 4.9 | 4.5 | 7.5 | 8.8 | 3.6 |
| Mississippi | 46.6 | 26.2 | 27.2 | 28.8 | 32.2 | 4.7 | 10.7 | 10.7 | 2.1 | 8.7 | 11.7 | 4.0 |
| Missouri | 52.2 | 20.6 | 27.2 | 25.8 | 28.0 | 4.7 | 8.6 | 6.8 | 4.2 | 12.4 | 10.3 | 3.6 |
| Montana | 49.3 | 24.6 | 26.1 | 28.8 | 28.4 | 3.6 | 10.4 | 7.0 | 5.7 | 13.8 | 13.5 | 2.4 |
| Nebraska | 57.9 | 22.2 | 19.9 | 24.1 | 22.1 | 2.1 | 8.0 | 4.6 | 3.7 | 10.1 | 9.5 | 3.0 |
| Nevada | 47.6 | 27.4 | 25.0 | 29.3 | 29.1 | 4.4 | 7.8 | 6.3 | 7.1 | 6.6 | 10.0 | 4.1 |
| New Hampshire | 57.5 | 22.8 | 19.7 | 20.0 | 23.7 | 3.6 | 4.5 | 4.1 | 2.2 | 9.1 | 9.0 | 1.5 |
| New Jersey | 58.6 | 23.3 | 18.1 | 23.3 | 21.1 | 2.4 | 4.5 | 4.0 | 2.7 | 6.3 | 7.0 | 3.4 |
| New Mexico | 46.7 | 25.5 | 27.8 | 24.9 | 31.5 | 4.6 | 11.8 | 11.1 | 6.2 | 11.5 | 12.6 | 5.3 |
| New York | 54.7 | 30.3 | 15.0 | 26.0 | 19.6 | 2.6 | 3.8 | 3.8 | 2.5 | 5.4 | 5.2 | 2.5 |
| North Carolina | 50.4 | 25.8 | 23.8 | 29.6 | 25.7 | 3.4 | 9.9 | 6.5 | 3.6 | 8.2 | 9.8 | 5.9 |
| North Dakota | 60.1 | 24.1 | 15.8 | 20.3 | 21.9 | 3.4 | 5.7 | 3.3 | 3.1 | 7.6 | 7.2 | 1.6 |
| Ohio | 50.5 | 22.4 | 27.1 | 31.1 | 27.7 | 4.4 | 11.1 | 8.1 | 5.3 | 9.3 | 10.7 | 2.1 |
| Oklahoma | 46.3 | 27.1 | 26.6 | 31.8 | 28.9 | 3.7 | 11.7 | 6.4 | 5.1 | 9.8 | 9.9 | 4.2 |
| Oregon | 52.7 | 24.9 | 22.4 | 28.6 | 24.8 | 2.0 | 7.0 | 6.1 | 3.0 | 10.5 | 10.8 | 2.8 |
| Pennsylvania | 52.9 | 25.9 | 21.2 | 23.5 | 25.7 | 3.8 | 8.6 | 5.5 | 4.3 | 10.0 | 8.5 | 2.8 |
| Rhode Island | 54.2 | 24.3 | 21.5 | 24.9 | 25.8 | 4.1 | 6.4 | 5.4 | 6.8 | 10.1 | 8.2 | 3.2 |
| South Carolina | 51.7 | 23.0 | 25.3 | 29.7 | 27.1 | 3.4 | 8.4 | 5.2 | 3.6 | 6.5 | 9.1 | 2.4 |
| South Dakota | 54.4 | 23.6 | 22.0 | 25.0 | 24.5 | 0.7 | 9.9 | 6.1 | 3.6 | 8.4 | 12.1 | 5.9 |
| Tennessee | 51.9 | 23.5 | 24.6 | 26.0 | 26.8 | 3.3 | 12.8 | 6.3 | 4.0 | 8.0 | 11.2 | 3.0 |
| Texas | 50.3 | 25.9 | 23.9 | 28.4 | 27.2 | 3.7 | 9.2 | 7.4 | 4.0 | 6.9 | 11.0 | 4.7 |
| Utah | 59.0 | 24.1 | 16.9 | 24.2 | 18.0 | 1.3 | 6.0 | 4.5 | 2.8 | 11.7 | 9.1 | 1.4 |
| Vermont | 55.0 | 25.1 | 19.9 | 25.1 | 23.5 | 3.5 | 5.6 | 4.5 | 3.0 | 11.2 | 12.2 | 1.6 |
| Virginia | 58.8 | 21.9 | 19.3 | 22.8 | 22.0 | 3.6 | 8.5 | 5.5 | 3.4 | 7.7 | 7.8 | 3.7 |
| Washington | 57.5 | 23.2 | 19.3 | 22.8 | 23.5 | 1.5 | 5.5 | 4.3 | 2.2 | 10.7 | 10.2 | 2.5 |
| West Virginia | 47.6 | 26.3 | 26.1 | 32.6 | 31.1 | 5.0 | 8.7 | 7.4 | 2.8 | 11.5 | 11.3 | 2.9 |
| Wisconsin | 58.6 | 21.2 | 20.3 | 23.2 | 22.2 | 2.6 | 9.1 | 5.7 | 4.4 | 8.7 | 8.5 | 3.5 |
| Wyoming | 53.3 | 20.7 | 26.0 | 27.4 | 25.9 | 3.1 | 9.0 | 8.0 | 2.9 | 12.1 | 11.6 | 3.0 |
| **United States** | **53.7%** | **24.6%** | **21.7%** | **25.4%** | **25.0%** | **3.3%** | **8.2%** | **5.7%** | **3.9%** | **7.8%** | **9.0%** | **3.7%** |

Source: 2016 National Survey of Children's Health. 2017. "Indicator 6.13: Adverse Childhood Experiences." Data Resource Center for Child & Adolescent Health. http://www.childhealthdata.org/browse/survey/results?q=4576&r=1.

## In 2014, more than 1 million children were arrested in the U.S. In six states more than 5 percent of children were arrested.

### Table 34: Child Arrests, 2014

| | Total Number of Child Arrests | Arrests per 100,000 Children 10–17 | Property Offense Arrests per 100,000 Children 10–17 |
|---|---|---|---|
| Alabama | 144 | n/a | n/a |
| Alaska | 1,863 | n/a | n/a |
| Arizona | 29,904 | 4,025 | 835 |
| Arkansas | 9,231 | 2,897 | 747 |
| California | 86,638 | 2,044 | 448 |
| Colorado | 30,570 | 5,487 | 1,093 |
| Connecticut | 9,499 | 2,482 | 502 |
| Delaware | 4,175 | 4,459 | 1,000 |
| District of Columbia | 332 | n/a | n/a |
| Florida | 66,839 | n/a | n/a |
| Georgia | 37,371 | 3,295 | 860 |
| Hawaii | 590 | n/a | n/a |
| Idaho | 9,360 | 4,848 | 936 |
| Illinois | 16,779 | n/a | n/a |
| Indiana | 15,814 | n/a | n/a |
| Iowa | 13,822 | 4,230 | 1,166 |
| Kansas | 5,106 | n/a | n/a |
| Kentucky | 6,496 | 1,418 | 476 |
| Louisiana | 19,723 | 3,965 | 1,017 |
| Maine | 3,925 | 3,115 | 755 |
| Maryland | 24,505 | 3,960 | 1,026 |
| Massachusetts | 9,186 | 1,386 | 242 |
| Michigan | 20,595 | 1,917 | 496 |
| Minnesota | 23,795 | 4,136 | 948 |
| Mississippi | 5,277 | n/a | n/a |
| Missouri | 24,765 | 3,884 | 868 |

| | | | |
|---|---|---|---|
| Montana | 4,981 | 4,943 | 1,075 |
| Nebraska | 12,293 | 6,075 | 1,598 |
| Nevada | 10,991 | 3,620 | 724 |
| New Hampshire | 4,800 | 3,561 | 487 |
| New Jersey | 24,307 | 2,570 | 387 |
| New Mexico | 7,787 | 3,435 | 772 |
| New York | 24,703 | 1,261 | 346 |
| North Carolina | 30,768 | 2,946 | 773 |
| North Dakota | 3,982 | 5,788 | 954 |
| Ohio | 24,585 | n/a | n/a |
| Oklahoma | 13,901 | 3,332 | 816 |
| Oregon | 7,249 | n/a | n/a |
| Pennsylvania | 62,170 | 4,884 | 587 |
| Rhode Island | 2,947 | 2,882 | 567 |
| South Carolina | 15,697 | 3,186 | 802 |
| South Dakota | 4,681 | 5,258 | 1,056 |
| Tennessee | 26,689 | 3,897 | 797 |
| Texas | 82,483 | 2,598 | 638 |
| Utah | 17,380 | 4,531 | 1,015 |
| Vermont | 686 | 1,152 | 212 |
| Virginia | 23,814 | 2,827 | 500 |
| Washington | 17,355 | 2,410 | 704 |
| West Virginia | 1,247 | n/a | n/a |
| Wisconsin | 56,054 | 9,291 | 1,745 |
| Wyoming | 4,144 | 7,050 | 1,126 |
| **United States** | **1,024,000** | **3,084** | **705** |

Notes: "n/a" means the state had a data coverage rate of less than 90 percent. "Property" offense includes "burglary, larceny-theft, motor vehicle theft, and arson."

Sources: Puzzanchera, Charles, and Wei Kang. 2014. "Easy Access to FBI Arrest Statistics 1994-2014." http://www.ojjdp.gov/ojstatbb/ezaucr/; Federal Bureau of Investigation. "Crime in the United States 2014." https://ucr.fbi.gov/crime-in-the-u.s/2014/crime-in-the-u.s.-2014/tables/table-69.

The State of America's Children® in

# WISCONSIN

2017 Factsheet

## Child Population

- **1,287,693** children lived in Wisconsin in 2016.
- **29 percent** were children of color: 9 percent were Black; 12 percent were Hispanic; 4 percent were Asian; and 1 percent were American Indian/Alaska Native.

## Child Poverty

- **16 percent** of Wisconsin's children were poor in 2016–a total of **198,480** children–and children of color were disproportionately poor.
- **43 percent** of Black, **28 percent** of Hispanic and **10 percent** of White children were poor.
- **7 percent** of children were extremely poor (their family had income at less than half the poverty level).
- **19 percent** of children under 6 were poor.

## Income and Wealth Inequality

- **$79,400** was the median income for White families with children compared with **$26,700** for Black and **$35,800** for Hispanic families in 2015.

## Housing and Homelessness

- **18,366** homeless children were enrolled in public schools during 2014-2015.
- **2.2 full-time jobs** at minimum wage were needed for a family to afford a two-bedroom rental unit at fair market rent in 2016.

## Child Hunger and Nutrition

- **17 percent** of children lived in food-insecure households in 2015.
- **30 percent** of children 10-17 were overweight or obese in 2016.
- **23 percent** relied on the Supplemental Nutrition Assistance Program (SNAP) in FY2015.
- **86 percent** of children receiving free or reduced-price lunch during the school year did not participate in Summer Nutrition Programs in 2016.

## Child Health

- **45,408** children 0-17 were uninsured in 2016.
- **712,697** children 0-18 were enrolled in Medicaid and BadgerCare Plus (Children's Health Insurance Program).

## Early Childhood

- **$11,750** was the average annual cost for an infant in center-based child care in 2015.
- **71 percent** of 4-year-olds were enrolled in state-funded preschool during 2015-2016.

## Education

- **89 percent** of Black, **81 percent** of Hispanic and **56 percent** of White 4th grade public school students could not read at grade level in 2015.
- **90 percent** of Black, **76 percent** of Hispanic and **55 percent** of White 8th grade public school students could not read at grade level in 2015.
- **64 percent** of Black, **78 percent** of Hispanic and **93 percent** of White students graduated high school on time during 2014-2015.
- **34 percent** of Black, **11 percent** of Hispanic and **4 percent** of White public secondary students had at least one out-of-school suspension in 2011-2012.

## Child Welfare

- **4,840** children were abused or neglected in 2015.
- **7,382** children were in foster care on the last day of FY2016.

## Juvenile Justice

- **762** children were in residential placement in 2015. **56 percent** were Black; **9 percent** were Hispanic; and **28 percent** were White.
- **37** children were in adult jails or prisons in 2015.

## Gun Violence

- **45** children and teens (3.1 per 100,000) were killed with a gun in 2015.

**Note:** All numbers in this factsheet are included in the Children's Defense Fund's *The State of America's Children®* 2017 report, and most have been rounded to the nearest whole number. Facts for states and the District of Columbia were omitted when data were not available. Citations for all data may be found in *The State of America's Children®* 2017.

# ACTION PLAN OUTLINE: